STARTING DESIGN & TECHNOLOGY

ELECTRONICS

JOHN CAVE

Series editor: John Cave

CASSELL

Cassell Publishers Limited
Artillery House
Artillery Row
London SW1P 1RT

First published 1989

ISBN 0-304-31647-4

Typeset by Flairplan Typesetting Ltd., Ware, Herts.

Printed and bound in Great Britain at The Bath Press, Avon.

Contents

The symbols used in this book are those in British Standards
3939, part 5. Where there is a choice, the most popular symbol
has been chosen.

Introduction

This book invites you into the fascinating world of electronics. Many people think this subject is hard and a bit mysterious, but if you read on you will find yourself doing electronics – and enjoying it.

To get the most from this book, try not to skip pages, and have a go at all the activities. All the words that will be new to you are printed in **bold** to start with and are listed in a mini-dictionary at the back. This will give you more information and help you to answer any questions. There are also sections on fault finding, product model making and, if you want, some simple mathematics.

One of the best ways of learning electronics is by designing and making things, and this book will guide you step by step through many different projects. All the materials and parts needed cost only a few pence and if you cannot get them all from school, they are readily available from a high street electronics supply shop.

Fact File

If we were able to shrink Nelson's Column (37 metres high) as much as computers have shrunk during the last 30 years, it would now slip into your pocket!

5

The Electronics Revolution

Why Is Electronics Important?

You have probably heard the term 'electronics revolution'. We talk about a revolution when changes happen very quickly – and it may surprise you to know that only in your own lifetime have computers become household items.

Looking back even further, the best machine for playing back recorded music 60 years ago used a large horn to **amplify**, or make louder, the sound when a needle vibrated its way through the grooves of a record. Modern records still have sound locked up in the form of wavy grooves, but we now have electronic amplifiers.

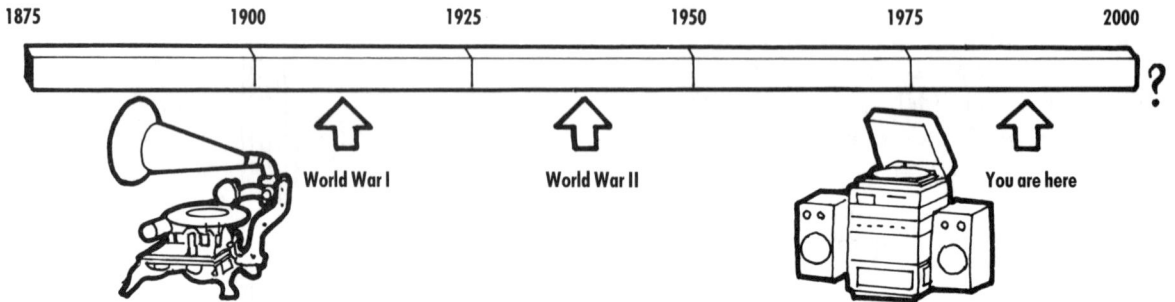

| 1875 | 1900 | 1925 | 1950 | 1975 | 2000 |

World War I   World War II   You are here

Experiment 1

If you want an idea of what records sounded like before electronics, take any *old* record and spin it around a pen with a finger while a friend lowers on to it a pin stuck through the end of a Sellotaped paper cone.

With a modern stereo system, we now hear sound with few of the hisses and scratches you may have just heard. This is just one example of the way electronics has changed our world.

Electronic Components

What Is Electronics?

All materials are made up of countless numbers of atoms, each of which is made up of smaller particles. One of these is the **electron**, and when large numbers of these are made to move through certain materials, we talk about an electric current flowing.

There are billions of electrons in the ink of this full stop.

Electronics is to do with managing and controlling these electrons in a **circuit**, which consists of different parts, or **components**, connected together. Making a television, radio or computer involves putting the right components together in the correct way.

A modern electronic circuit.

As in all subjects, you have to walk before you can run, and this book will show you, in turn, just a handful of the most important components in electronics. Even so, you will be amazed at how many things you can design and make with them.

These are the components you will be working with:

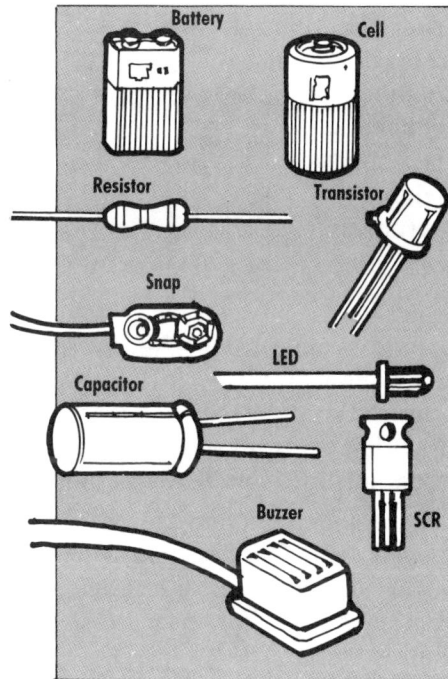

1 Batteries

Because current cannot be seen, many people find it helpful to think of it as something like water flowing in a pipe.

The **dry cell** is one way of producing current. We think of it as a kind of pump that uses chemicals rather than a mechanism. The chemicals inside are not doing much until something that passes, or **conducts**, current is connected between the (+) and (−) terminals.

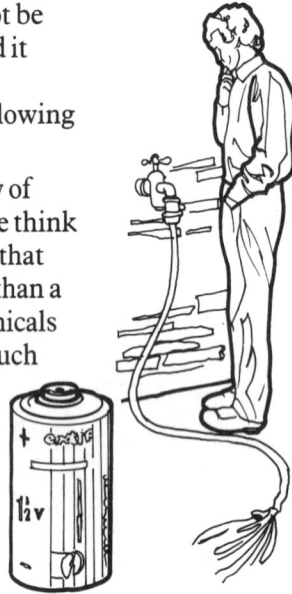

If a small bulb is connected in that way, the cell pumps electrons out from (−) to flow through the wire and the very fine bulb filament and back to (+). The electrons *must return* to the cell, so there must be a complete wire loop.

In this very simple circuit (most torches use it), the filament of the bulb is designed to obstruct, or **resist**, the flow of current. When this happens, it gets hot – so hot, in fact, that it glows white.

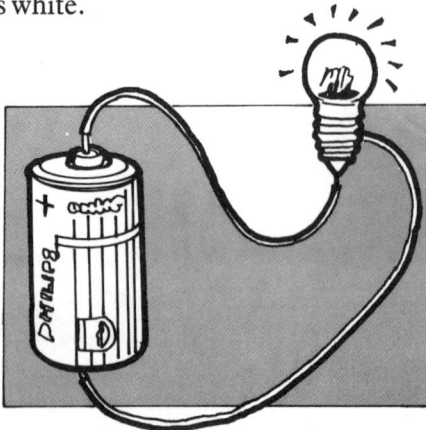

Although we know that electrons flow from (−) to (+), many years ago it was thought that current was a kind of fluid and flowed from (+) to (−). This is known as **conventional current flow**, and it is common to speak of electricity flowing in this direction.

Fact File

Did you know that any torch bulb filament gets hotter than molten gold or silver?

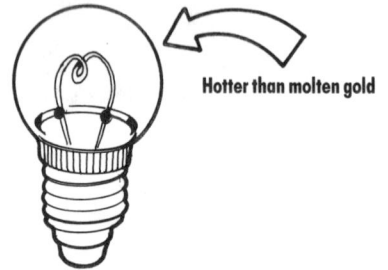

Hotter than molten gold

It might help you to think of the circuit as a water pump with a kinked hose-pipe connecting the output ($-$) and the input ($+$). Just as the chemicals in the dry cell work to move current through the filament, so the pump does the same job, forcing water through the pipe and its kink.

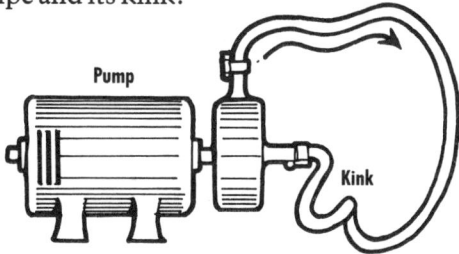

We measure the quantity of current flowing in a circuit in units called **amps** (A). Since these are very large for most electronics work, we tend to use milliamps (mA). 1mA = 1/1000th of an amp.

Pressure in a circuit is measured in **volts** (V) and the dry cell has a pressure, or voltage, of roughly 1.5V. If a number of cells are linked together ($+$) to ($-$) as shown, we end up with the familiar **battery**. Each cell added increases the pressure or voltage by 1.5 V.

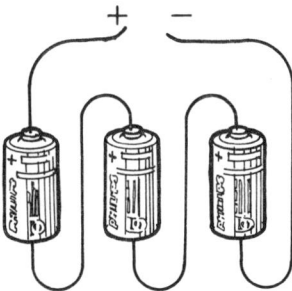

Circuit Diagrams

In the very early days of electronics, circuits were drawn with pictures of the components. This becomes confusing in a large diagram, so we now use **symbols** for the components and straight lines for wires. These are drawn either in parallel or at right angles to each other.

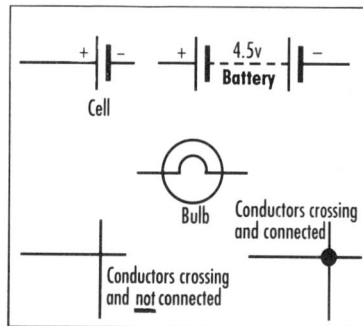

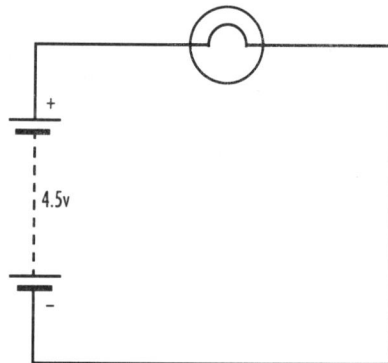

Circuit diagram of bulb connected to 4.5 V battery.

Fact File

Some fish have their own batteries, made up of so many cells that they can give an electric shock of hundreds of volts.

2 The LED and Resistor

The LED

Most of the circuits in this book use a **light emitting diode** (**LED**) rather than a bulb. LEDs give out less light, but they use less current and *cost less*. LEDs also come in three colours: red, green and amber.

Unlike a bulb, an LED does not have a filament. It is too hard to explain here how it works, but it is easy to use if you follow two simple rules:

Symbol for LED

LED Rule 1

An LED must be used with a **resistor** in the circuit loop. This restricts current flow and prevents the LED taking more current than is good for it. More is said about resistors below, but for now we can apply an easy 'rule of thumb' (a rough rule) for the resistor value. Its resistance, measured in **ohms** (Ω), should be about 50Ω per volt of battery voltage. For a 9V battery, it should be 9 $\times 50 = 450\Omega$ (or near to it).

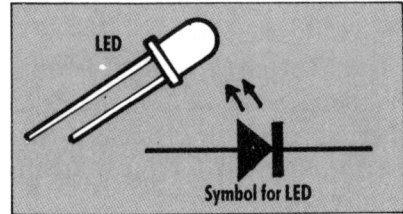

Symbol for resistor

LED Rule 2

An LED must be connected in a circuit with its $(-)$ leg facing towards the $(-)$ terminal of the battery. If you look on the bottom of an LED, there is a small *flat edge* on the plastic, and the $(-)$ leg is nearest to this.

An LED is a **diode**. This lets current pass only when it is connected in a circuit the right way around. If it is connected backwards, nothing happens – and no light!

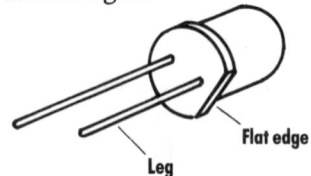

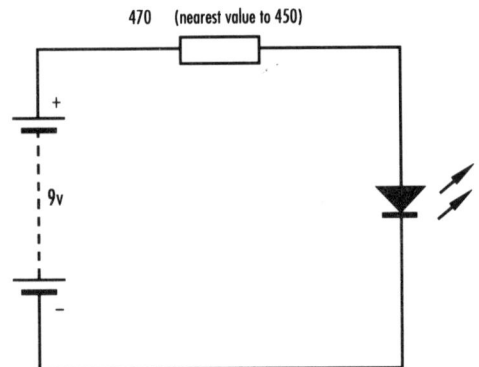

Flat edge

Leg

Circuit diagram of LED and resistor connected to battery.

The Resistor

Resistors

Resistors are very important in electronics because we often have to limit the amount of current flowing in a circuit – or parts of it. The most common resistors consist of a thin film of **carbon** over a **ceramic** tube, each end of which has a wire connecting leg. The resistance simply depends on the type of carbon used.

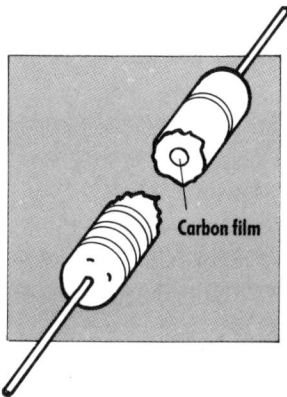

Carbon film

Resistors are colour coded with four bands that can be read to give their value in ohms (Ω). The higher the number in ohms, the greater the resistance.

To read a resistor's value, look at its first colour band (opposite end to the metallic band) and find this colour on the chart. Now look *across* the chart to Column 1 and note the number. Do this for the other two colour bands, going across the chart to Column 2 and then to Column 3.

If, for example, the resistor's first colour band is yellow, we note '4' in Column 1 on the chart. If the second band is violet, we go across to Column 2 and note '7'. If the third is red, we see two noughts in Column 3, giving a figure of 4,700. This is the value in ohms of the resistor.

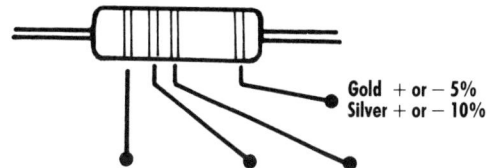

Gold + or − 5%
Silver + or − 10%

Colour	Band 1	Band 2	Band 3
Black	0	0	Nothing
Brown	1	1	0
Red	2	2	00
Orange	3	3	000
Yellow	4	4	0000
Green	5	5	00000
Blue	6	6	000000
Violet	7	7	
Grey	8	8	
White	9	9	

The LED and Resistor

Resistors in Series

A resistor is never perfect, and the metallic end band tells us how accurate it is. Silver means + or − 10 per cent of the coded value, so if we read that the resistor is 100Ω (brown, black, brown), it could actually be anything between 110Ω and 95Ω. A gold band means + or − 5 per cent, and so our 100Ω resistor would be between 105Ω and 95Ω.

To save having to write lots of noughts, there is an abbreviation for thousands of ohms (K) and for millions (M). For example, a 1,000Ω resistor (brown, black, red) is called 1K and a 1,000,000Ω resistor (brown, black, green) is called 1M. A decimal point can also be used:

for example 4.7K is 4,700
                 4.7M is 4,700,000.

But, it is more usual now to use the K and M in place of the decimal point, giving: 4K7 for 4,700 and 4M7 for 4,700,000.

Manufacturers make resistors only in certain values, called preferred values, but we can join them up in **series** or **parallel** to give many more. Each resistor in a series restricts current, *increasing* the resistance from A to B. You just add the values together to get a total.

Total Resistance is 1K + 1K = 2K

You need to think harder about resistors connected in parallel. Giving the current two or more paths from A to B makes the total resistance *less*! For the mathematically minded, the total resistance is given by

$$\frac{1}{R} + \frac{1}{R} = \; \ldots \; \frac{1}{R}(\text{total})$$

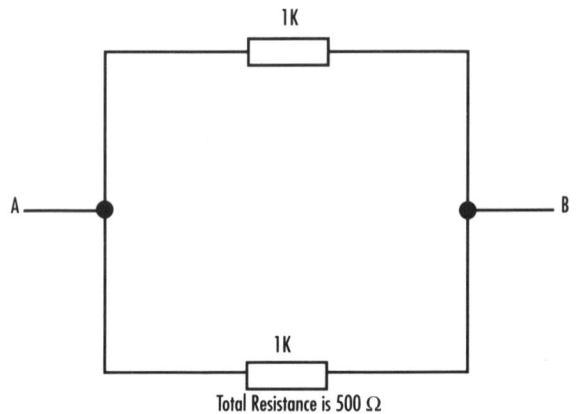

Total Resistance is 500 Ω

Questions

Test Yourself So Far

Before the first project, see if you can answer these questions. Look back over what you have read and use the Mini-Dictionary for help.

1 'Radio was invented after the Second World War.' True or false?
2 What is hotter than molten gold but will not burn a hole in your pocket?
3 Should the bulb shown in this diagram be lit up or not? Why?

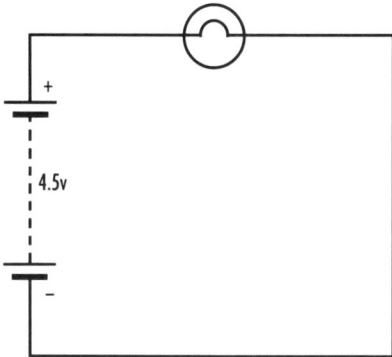

4 What is the total voltage if these cells are connected as shown?

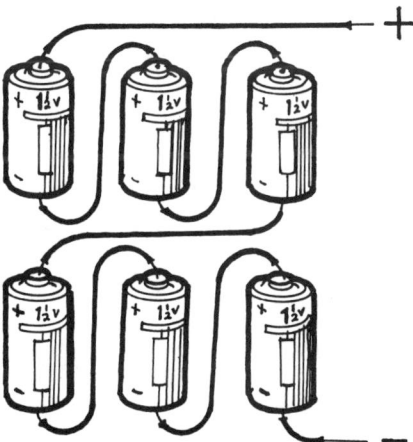

5 Will this work? Explain.

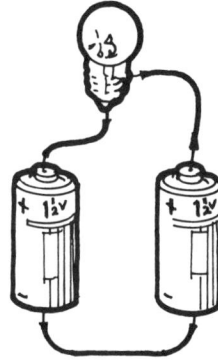

6 This circuit diagram contains many deliberate mistakes. How many can you spot?

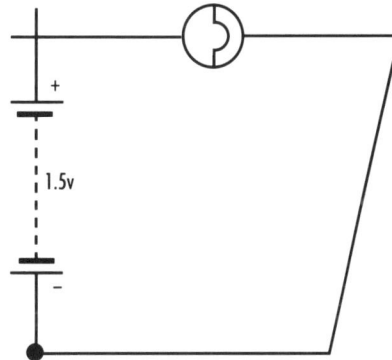

7 The LED in this circuit glows brightly for a couple of seconds and then goes out forever. Why?

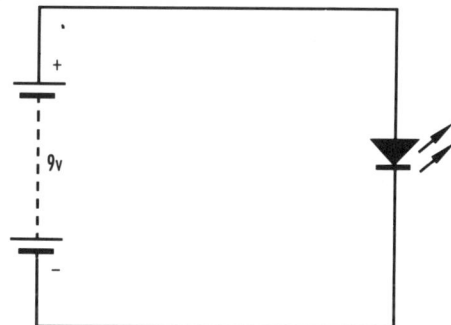

13

The LED and Resistor

Questions

8 Neither of these circuits works. Why not?

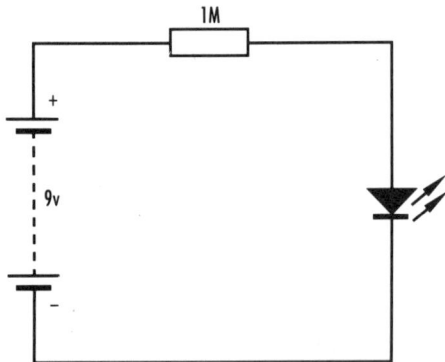

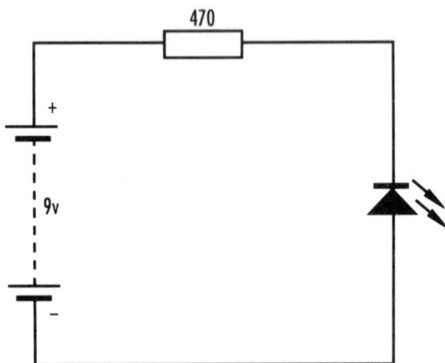

9 What are the coded values of these resistors?

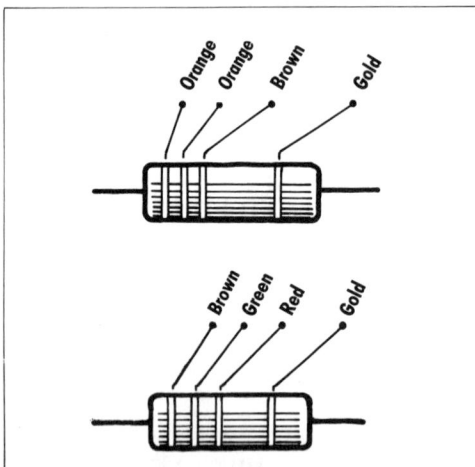

10 What would be the *total* value of the resistors if connected as shown?

11 What would be the total value of these two resistors if connected as shown?

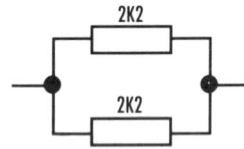

Fact File

- Did you know that the **graphite** 'lead' in a pencil conducts current and can be used as a resistor? A 4H pencil has a higher resistance than a 4B because clay is mixed with the graphite to make it harder.
- You can actually make resistors just by drawing them on paper with a soft pencil, but they are likely to have a high resistance!

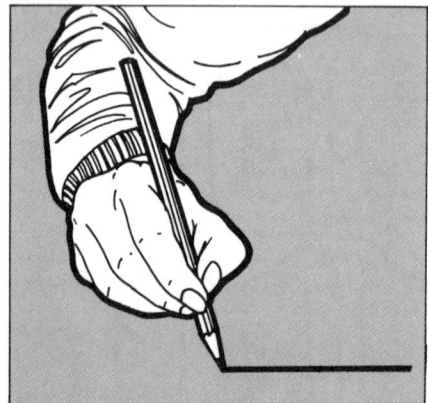

Making a Compression Joint Circuit

Project 1: Making a Circuit

Strange as it may seem, the LED and resistor circuit, with just two components, has hundreds of uses: from checking the wiring on Concorde to making sure pot plants are properly watered! We shall be looking at some of these uses, but first you must build the circuit.

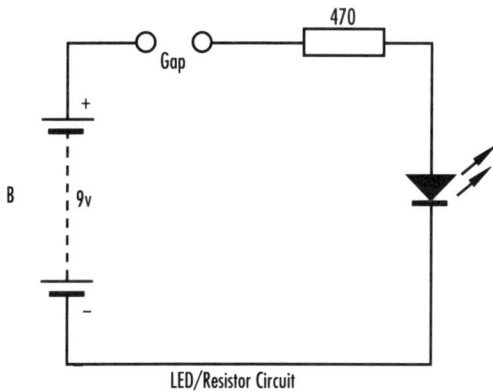

LED/Resistor Circuit

Components can be connected in many ways. Merely twisting the component legs and connecting wires around each other is messy and unreliable. Three much better ways are described here. Try Method 1 first. **All the circuits are shown constructed in this way, but either of the other two methods could be used.**

Method 1: Wedging with pins

Draw the circuit diagram on a block of softwood (80 × 80 × 20 mm) and drill holes where component legs and connecting wires meet. Use a 15 mm long panel pin, with its head cut off, as the drill bit. *Do not make the holes too big!*

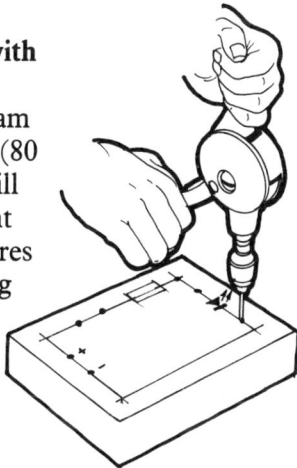

The connecting wires are cut to length and their ends stripped. These are bent over and dropped into the holes together with the component legs. Panel pins are tapped in to make a tight joint. The complete circuit shows a battery **snap** coming off the block at one end and two flying leads. The ends of these leads, if touched together, complete the circuit loop and light the LED.

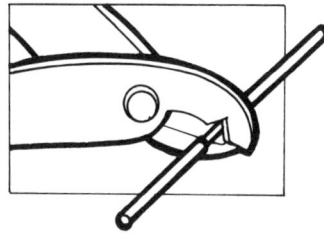

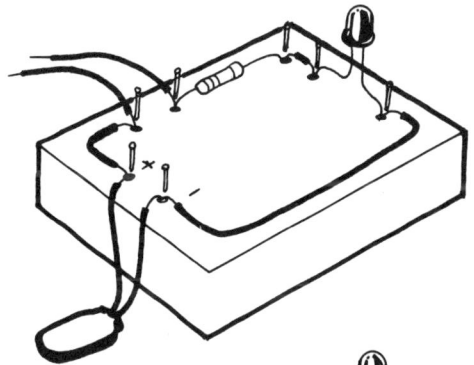

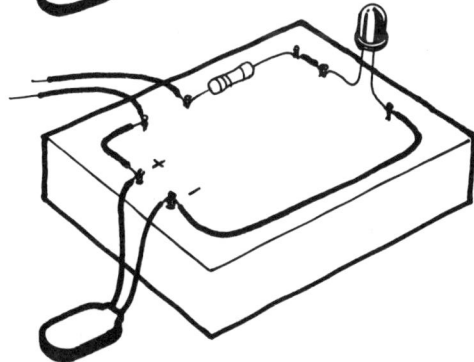

Note: Use single core wire on the board itself and flexible stranded wire for the flying leads.

The LED and Resistor

Making a Soldered Circuit

Method 2: Soldering on to pins
Solder is an alloy that can be melted with a hot soldering-iron to form a joint.

First, mark out a block of wood, as before, with the circuit diagram. Instead of drilling holes, tap in brass-plated panel pins with their heads about 4 mm above the surface.

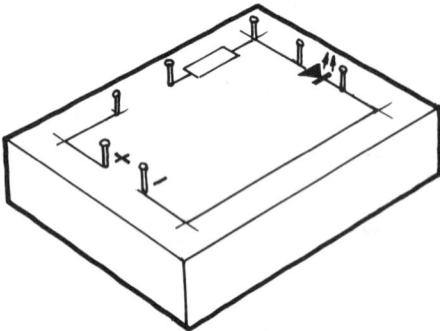

Holding the soldering-iron in one hand and a length of solder in the other, heat up one of the pins and then touch the solder to it. As the solder melts, **flux** will run out of its centre, helping it to run and stick on to the pin. It is no use melting the solder on to the iron's tip and then offering it to the pin because the flux quickly vanishes as smoke.

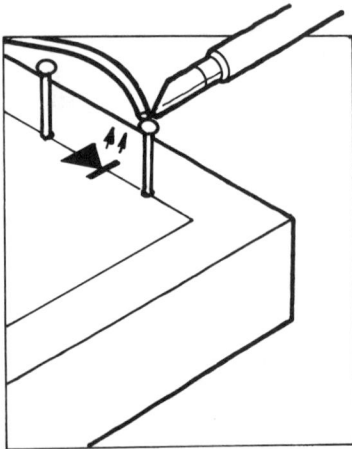

Coating with solder is called **tinning**. This must also be done to the other pins, the component legs and the stripped ends of the wires. You will probably find it helpful to use a *wooden* clothes-peg for holding wires and resistors while tinning. For other components, you should use a pair of pliers. These act as a **heat sink**, soaking up heat from the soldering-iron before it damages the component.

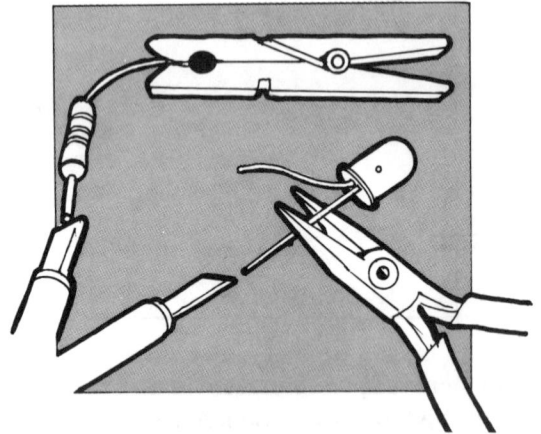

When tinning is completed, twist the legs and wires around their pins and re-heat with the soldering-iron, putting on more solder as needed and protecting the LED from heat damage.

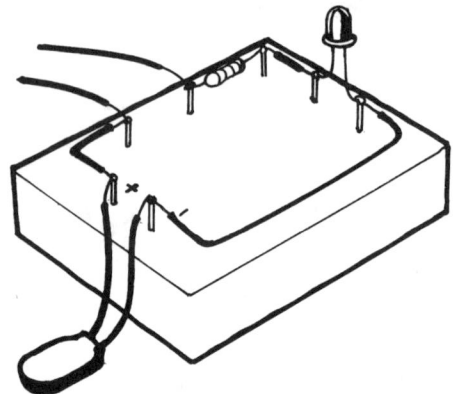

Making a Printed Circuit Board

Method 3: Printed circuit board (PCB)
This way of making circuits is the most common in electronics. Components are soldered between thin copper lines, or tracks, on a board instead of connecting wires. We shall be using **surface mounting**, which is explained later.

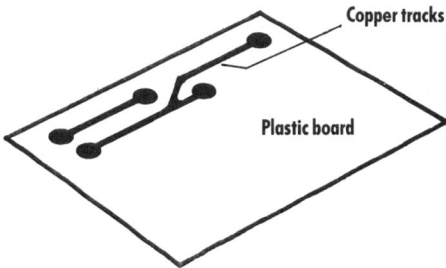

Printed circuit board.

To make a PCB, you will need:
1 Copper-clad board (40 × 40 mm). This is very thin copper sheet bonded to a plastic board.
2 A good spirit-based felt-tipped pen (medium tip).
3 Ferric chloride solution. **This is harmful. It should only be used when a teacher is in charge and you are wearing goggles.**

First mark out the tracks on the copper side of the board with pencil and then with the felt-tipped pen. The ink lines should be 2 to 3 mm wide and have fatter round ends. The components are soldered at these points, so more copper makes it less likely to pull off the board if a wire or component is knocked.

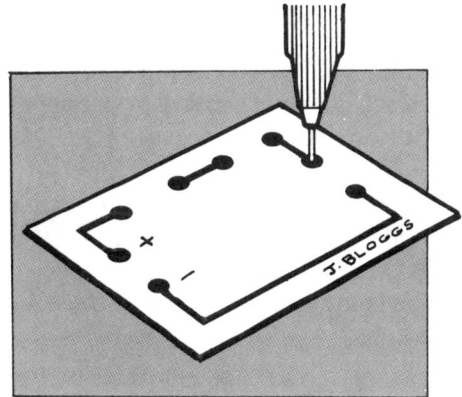

Next, the board is put into a *warm* ferric chloride solution. All the copper *not* covered by ink is eaten away. When ready, the board is washed and the ink removed with a solvent or wire wool.

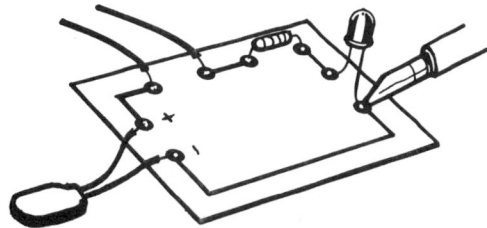

Finally, the LED and resistor legs are bent and tinned (together with the track ends) and soldered to the board.

Surface Mounting

Method of the future: Surface mounting

Up to a few years ago, most PCBs had components on top of the board with their legs going through holes and soldered to copper tracks underneath. This held them securely in place.

In surface mounting, the copper tracks are on the top side along with the components, which are much smaller and designed to sit flat on the board. Surface mounting resistors, for example, look like tiny bricks with metal end-caps. They are very difficult to place and solder on by hand. But you do not have to worry yet as the older wire-ended components will be around for some time and can be surface mounted!

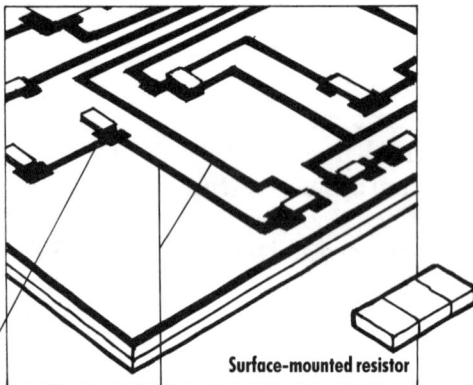

Surface-mounted resistor

Surface-mounted components shown full size   Copper tracks

Many professional circuit designers now surface mount wire-ended components on their prototype circuit boards. It is important to make sure, however, that larger components are secure.

Experiment 2

Now the first circuit is complete, you can use it for finding out which materials conduct current and which **insulate**. Bridge across the flying leads with a conductor and the LED glows brightly as the circuit loop is completed.

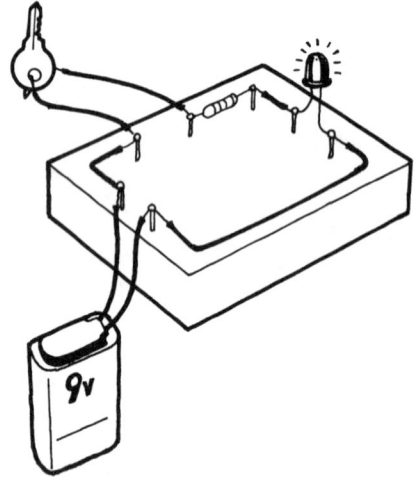

Insulators will have no effect, but some materials behave like resistors and let through just enough current to make the LED glow faintly.

Test the things shown and record your results in three columns with the headings: *Conductor*, *Insulator*, *Part-Conductor*.

LED Projects

Project 2: Make a Bulb and Fuse Tester

The filament in a mains light bulb or the fine copper wire inside a fuse are not normally visible – and are sometimes 'blown'.

Your circuit can be used to find out if a bulb or fuse is good by connecting it across the flying leads.

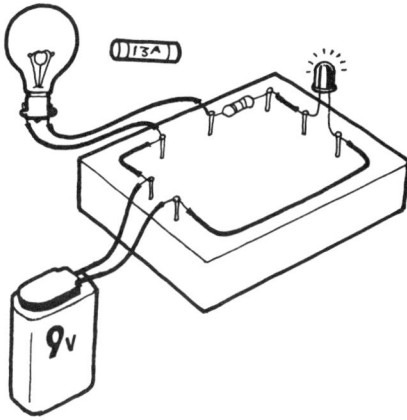

Using the LED circuit, can you design and make a bulb and fuse tester in one? It should not be too heavy or large and you should be able just to touch on bulbs or fuses to test them.

These are the measurements for the gap between light bulb terminals and fuse ends.

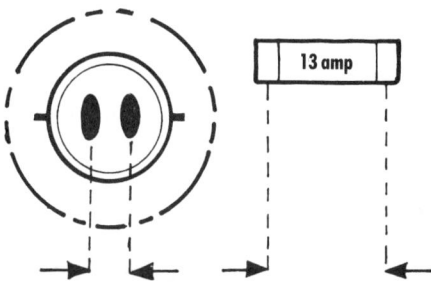

Project 3: Design a Pot-Plant Monitor

Experiment 2 may have suggested that wet soil will conduct current. If you connect a pair of thin brass wires (probes) to your flying leads and push them into the soil of a pot plant (about 25 mm apart), the LED will glow if the soil is moist but not if dry.

Using the LED circuit, design and make a device that will enable gardeners to check quickly if their plants have been watered.

The monitor should not be too large or heavy and must be easy to handle. (Use a 9V PP3 battery and a 470Ω resistor.)

A monitor that has to be pushed on a trolley is not a good idea!

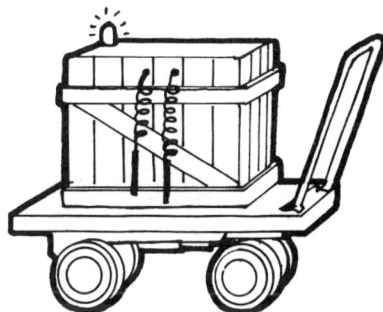

The LED and Resistor

LED Projects

Project 4: The Famous 5-Wire Puzzle

A very common problem in electronics is matching up the two ends of a long wire when most of it is hidden. Concorde and other aircraft have miles of wiring in them – as do British Telecom exchanges. In both cases, a circuit like the one you have made is used in a continuity test: one that tells you if there is a connection from A to B.

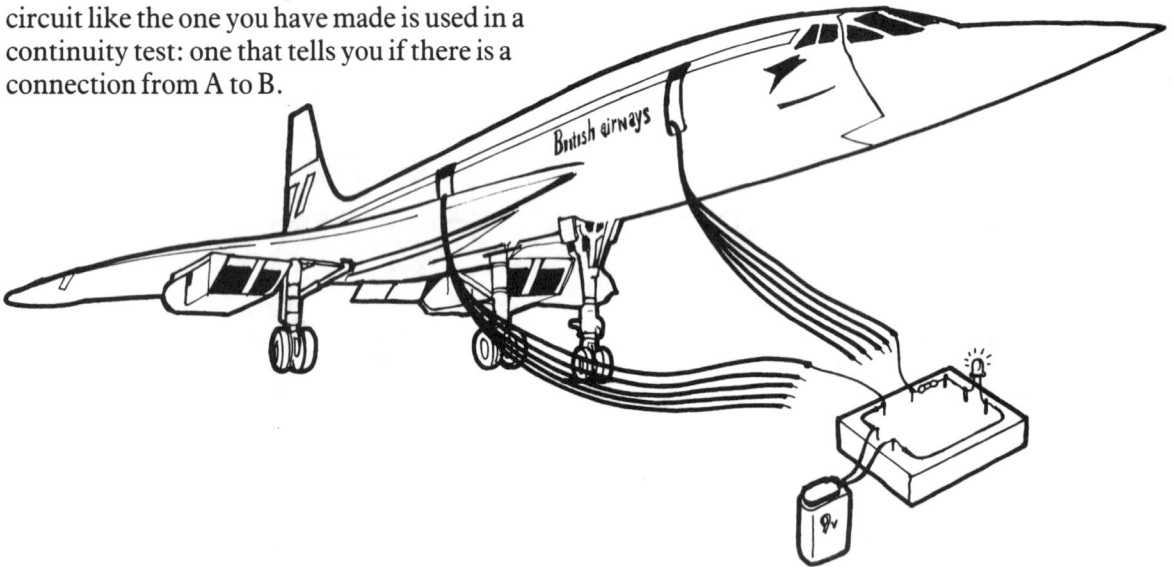

The 5-wire puzzle consists of five lengths of similar coloured wire, knotted in the middle so that it is not clear which end belongs to which. Using the LED circuit, the player works against the clock to match up the ends and clip the correct pairs together with paper-clips. The record time for the puzzle's solution is 10.5 seconds.

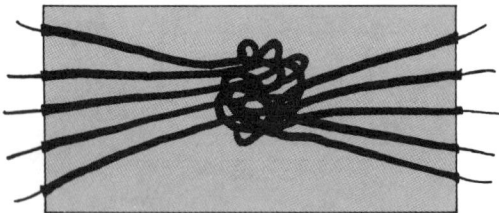

Can you design and make a more complicated version of this game? Different-coloured wires, for example, could be connected in the middle with a terminal block hidden in a tube or box. These could be changed every so often, a little bit like reprogramming a computer.

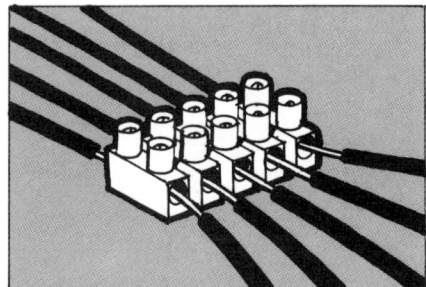

Because the earth is a good conductor of current, it was used in place of one wire in old telegraph and telephone circuits – saving quite a bit of money.

If you extend the flying leads of your first circuit and connect them to long probes, like very large nails, you can see for yourself how this worked.

Make sure the nails are well connected to the leads and put them into moist earth – at first close together and then further apart.

3 Switches and Membrane Panels

Types of Switch

Switches give us control over circuits by passing current, preventing its flow, or by changing its path. When a switch is *open* ('off' position), current cannot flow, and when *closed* ('on' position), it can.

Open   Closed

Switch symbol.

The knife switch (always used in Frankenstein horror films) was one of the earliest switches and although rarely used now, our modern symbol for a simple on/off switch looks very much like it.

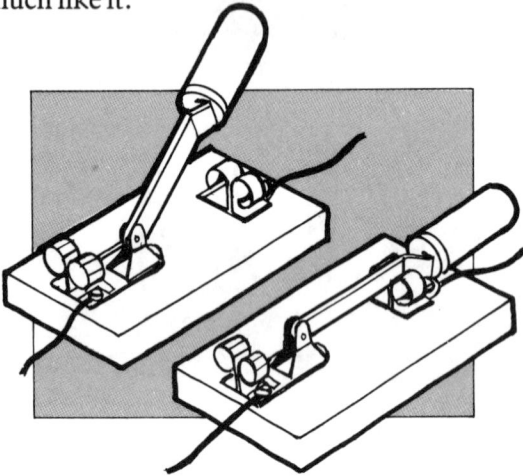

The symbol for a push-button switch also looks very like the inside of the original Victorian versions.

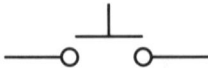

The switches we use now tend to be much smaller and are made mostly of plastics. They come in all shapes and sizes and are put to many different uses.

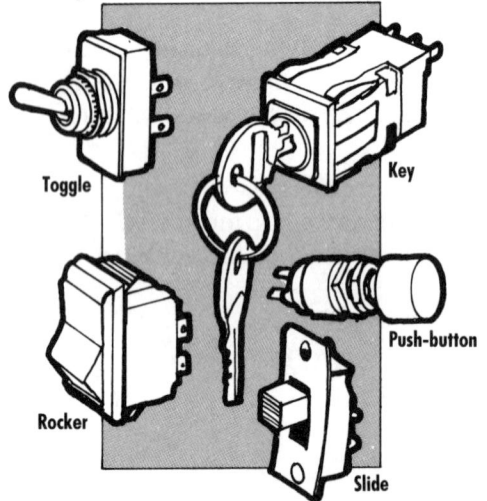

Toggle

Key

Rocker

Push-button

Slide

A newcomer to modern switches is the **membrane panel**. This uses thin, floppy, plastic sheets or layers in a sandwich rather than other moving parts. A very simple membrane-panel switch has three layers. Layer 1 has a pair of thin metal tracks. Layer 2 has a hole, or window, cut out and Layer 3 has a small metal patch in its centre, on the underside.

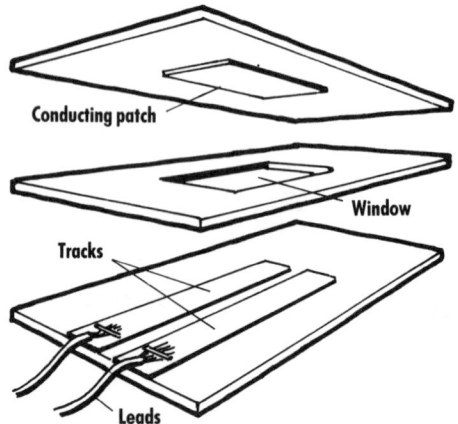

Conducting patch

Window

Tracks

Leads

The Membrane Panel

When all three layers are stuck together, the top metal patch is held away from the two bottom tracks by the thickness of the middle layer. But when the top is pressed, it dips through the window and touches across the two tracks, completing any circuit connected to them.

More complicated membrane panels also work in this way and can be found on such things as cash registers, videos and photocopiers.

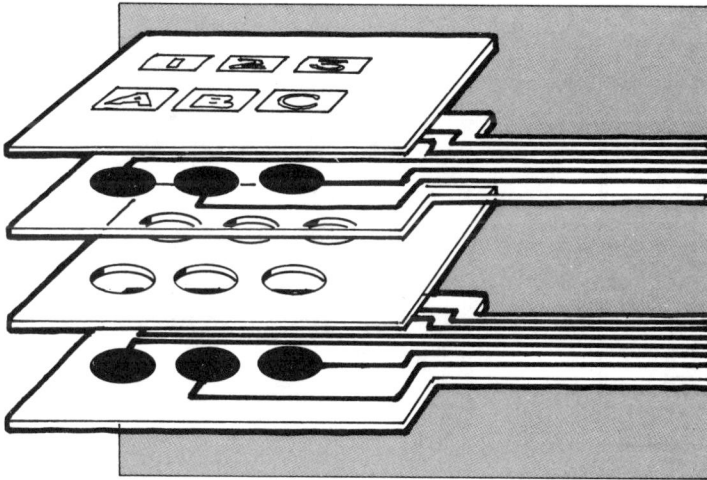

Fact File

When a light switch in your home is turned off, current tries to keep flowing and will jump across a small gap as a spark. The result is a burst of interference on your radio and television sets.

Making Membrane Panels

Project 5: Making a Membrane-Panel Switch

It is amazingly easy to make a membrane-panel switch. You only need the following:

- thick paper or thin card
- kitchen foil
- Sellotape
- PrittStick glue
- scissors
- stranded wire

First, cut three paper squares (100 × 100 mm) and make a hole in the middle of one, about 15 mm square. Cut two strips of foil about 10 mm wide and glue these to one sheet. Take care not to wrinkle the foil. Glue a foil patch (20 × 20 mm) in the centre of the third sheet.

Using stranded wires, spread out the stripped ends over the two foil tracks and tape them down firmly. If possible, staple the wire down as well, so that it is not so easy to tug off.

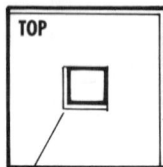

TOP

Foil patch

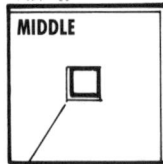

MIDDLE

Hole (15 mm × 15 mm)

BOTTOM

2 mm gap
Sellotape
Foil track

Finally, with small dots of glue, tack the three sheets together in a sandwich – and the switch is complete!

Test it with the LED circuit. If the LED stays lit, it means the patch is touching the tracks all the time. This is usually because of wrinkles in the foil. If nothing happens, it will almost certainly be because the wires are not making good contact with the tracks. Make sure they are pressed well down.

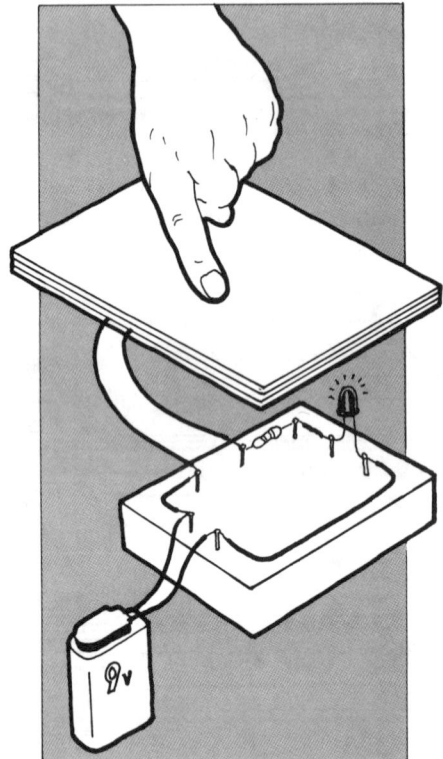

Making Membrane Panels

The appealing thing about membrane panels is that, just like the real thing, you can put bright graphics on the top. Felt pens, rub-down lettering, and even magazine cut-outs can all be used. When covered with self-adhesive bookcover film (matt if possible), they really look professional.

Project 6: Door Buzzer with Membrane Switch

There are many ways of announcing a visitor's arrival. They include shouting through the letter-box, banging on the door, or pressing a button. The last of these is probably best but most switches used with door buzzers or bells are difficult to see.

To get over this problem, you are asked to design and make a membrane-panel switch for a bell or buzzer. It is to be fastened to a door or door-frame and, as well as attracting the attention of the visitor, it has to fit in.

Points to think about:

1 Where will the switch be used – at the back or the front of the house? Is it to be serious or fun?
2 How will the switch be fixed on? Will it be fixed to an acrylic or wooden back?
3 What shape will the switch be? It does not have to be square!
4 What will be used for the graphics on the top?

Membrane-Panel Projects

Project 7: A Membrane Game

A different type of membrane-panel switch uses a complete covering of foil on the top and bottom layers, and has several windows in the middle one. Whenever the top is pushed through one of these windows, the foils touch to complete a circuit.

If a switch, roughly 150 mm square, is made up using paper/card and foil (with just a few windows), it can become a game where the players take it in turns to guess where the windows are.

An extra layer with graphics can be laid over the top – for example, a treasure map for younger children to guess where things are hidden. The extra layer might be a kind of Snakes and Ladders game where players move along a grid on the throw of a dice and have to move backwards when their counter lands on a window.

With this game, you keep the same switch but simply change the top layer. It is a little bit like programming a computer!

Using this type of membrane switch, can you design and make a game for two or more players?

Points to think about:

1. Do not make the windows too big; 15 mm square is about right if thick paper is used.
2. How will you prevent players feeling where the windows are? A thick top layer is one answer, but this might make the switch hard to use. A crafty designer might put in false windows and patches of thin paper to prevent contact.

Project 8: Mat Switch

The last membrane switch is also used in burglar alarms. It is called a 'mat switch' when the middle layer has windows all over the surface. Hidden under a carpet, contact is made through one or more of the windows when a burglar treads on it.

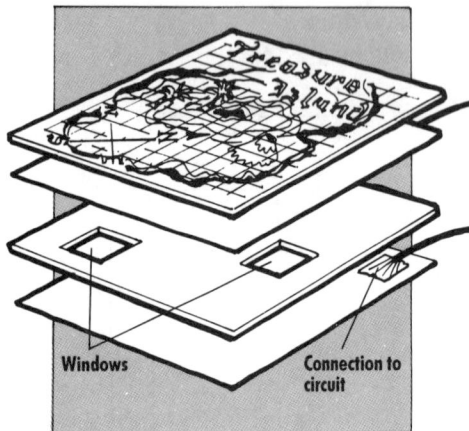

Windows

Connection to circuit

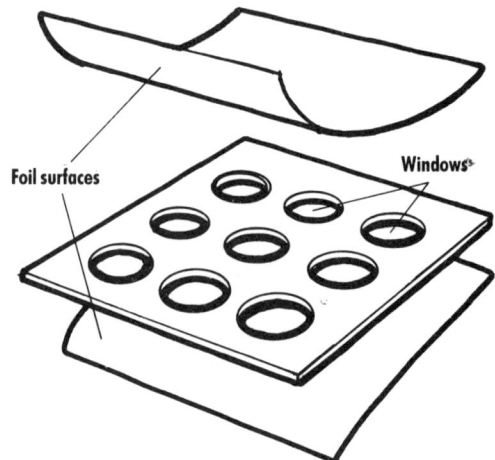

Foil surfaces

Windows

Membrane mat switch.

Membrane-Panel Projects

The problem with mat switches is that they are not always very sensitive. A burglar with big feet, whose weight is spread over a large area, might not cause the foil to dip right through any of the windows. On the other hand, a cat might just put one of its paws in the right place!

Using your LED circuit to test it, can you design and make a small mat switch for a burglar alarm? You will have to experiment with different materials and with the shape and number of windows.

4 The Capacitor

Finding out about Capacitors

Our only source of current so far has been the battery. It is very useful, though, to store current somewhere for a short time and release it when needed. This can be done using a **capacitor**. It is best to think of capacitors as a kind of tank or bucket for current.

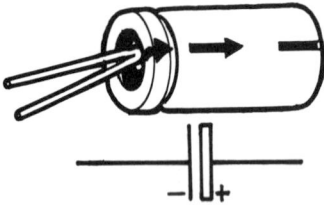

The unit of capacitance is the **farad** (F), but because this is so big, we will be working in micro-farads (μF), millionths of a farad.

The best way of getting to know the capacitor is to try an experiment with a large one. Take a 2,000 μF capacitor and touch its legs on to the terminals of a 9V PP3 battery, making sure that the leg marked (−) goes to (−) on the battery. The capacitor will fill or charge up in under a second! (*Warning:* Never exceed the voltage printed on the capacitor.)

Now connect the capacitor the *correct way round* to an LED and resistor. The LED will glow for about four seconds, and gradually dim as the capacitor runs out, or *discharges*.

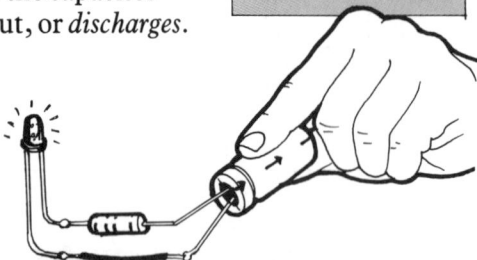

Sometimes very large capacitors are used to 'dump' big currents very quickly, and you can do this by charging up the capacitor and then touching its legs together. There will be a small spark as they touch, and even though tiny, it is hot enough to melt some of the metal on the legs. Much larger electrical sparks are used everyday to melt or weld metals together.

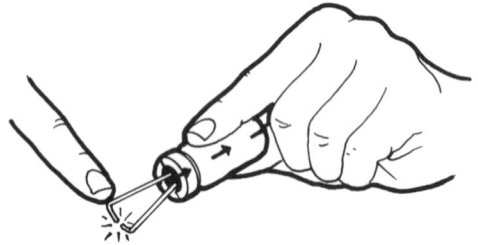

A much smaller capacitor, say 10μF, will not store enough current to light the LED, but you can experiment with a small loudspeaker; connecting a small charged capacitor to it produces a single sharp click.

Try some more experiments to answer these questions:
1 What happens if you use a higher value resistor in series with the LED?
2 What happens if two capacitors are put in parallel and used in the experiment?
3 How long is it before the capacitor's current just *leaks* away? Minutes, hours or days?

Finding out about Capacitors

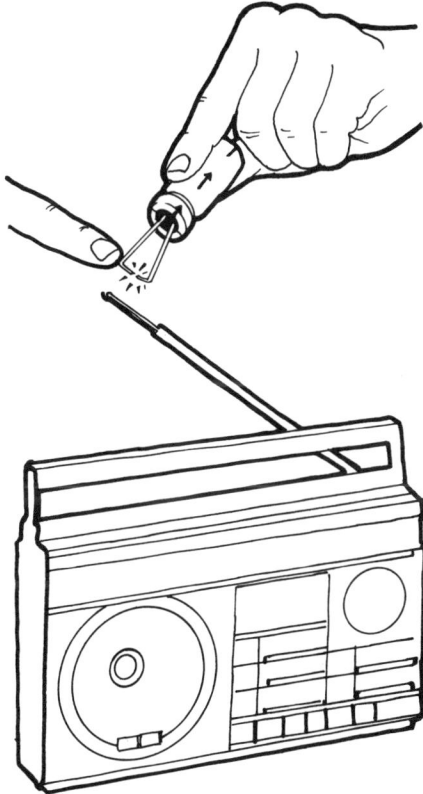

A large capacitor can be made up from a number of smaller ones by connecting these together in parallel. The total capacitance is the values of the small capacitors added together.

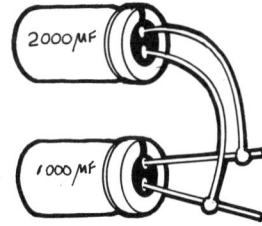

If we connected a 1000 µF capacitor and a 2000 µF capacitor together, their total capacitance would be:

$$1000\,\mu F + 2000\,\mu F = 3000\,\mu F.$$

When capacitors are added together to store more current, it is important to connect their legs as shown. The (−) legs (next to the markings on the cases) must be connected.

Capacitor Projects

Project 9: A Capacitor-Delay Circuit

Because it stores current, a capacitor can be added to the LED circuit to keep the LED on *after* current from the battery is stopped.

When the circuit is completed by touching the flying leads together, the LED comes on as before, but now the capacitor charges up as well.

After the leads are separated, the capacitor releases its current and acts like a battery, keeping the LED glowing for a few seconds. Just how long depends on the size of the capacitor and the value of the resistor.

The higher the value in each case, the longer the LED will stay on. For this reason, we overlook the rule of thumb (see page 10) and make the resistor a higher value.

The circuit is a very useful one because the LED glows for long enough to tell us there has been a very short contact. Without it, the LED would just flash on and then off and we might not even notice.

You now need to make up this circuit by one of the three methods so that it can be put to use in the next two projects.

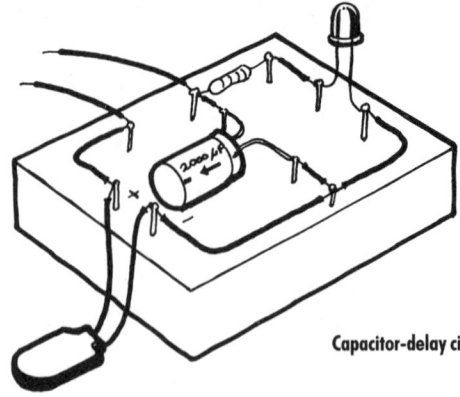

Capacitor-delay circuit.

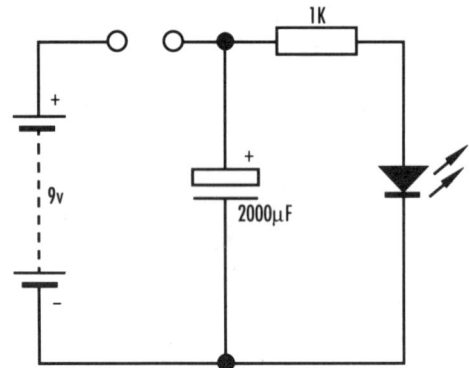

Circuit diagram of capacitor delay.

Fact File

The biggest capacitors ever made were used in early radio transmitters. The engineers could walk around *inside* them!

Capacitor Projects

Project 10: Electronic Wire Game

A popular challenge at fairgrounds and money-raising events is the game of skill that asks you to pass a small wire loop along a length of twisted wire without the two touching.

The electronics used for this is usually no more than our own LED circuit. The problem is that the two wires might make only a brief contact without the circuit clearly showing it.

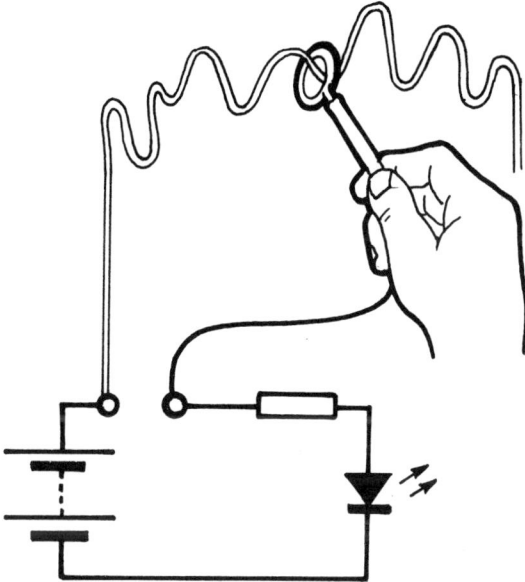

Using the capacitor for a delay, we have a solution to this problem because the LED stays on for a time even after the slightest contact.

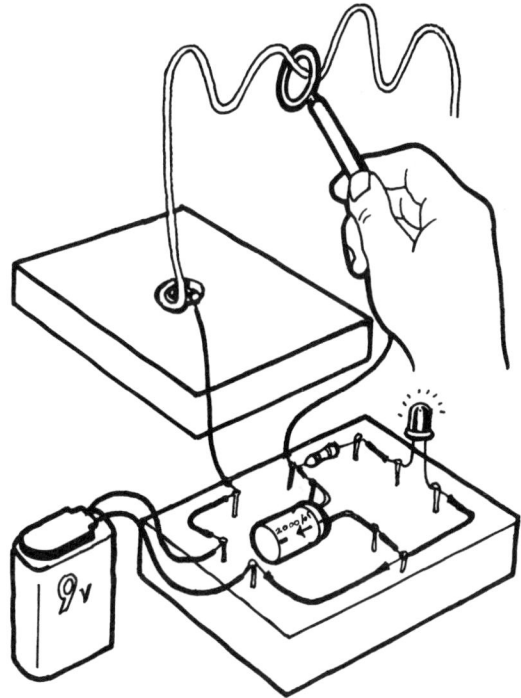

Using the capacitor-delay circuit, you are asked to design and make an electronic wire game for a school fund-raising event. You should be able to adjust it for different levels of skill.

Points to think about:

1 Will the game have a base *board*? Will it have some kind of frame? What materials will be used? Is the circuit on the base?
2 How are the stiff wires connected to the circuit leads? (Small terminal blocks are always useful.)
3 Can the wire loops be changed over – the smaller, the more difficult the game?

The Capacitor

Capacitor Projects

Project 11: Electronic Money-Box

A toymaker's notebook shows he is thinking about money-boxes for younger children. When money is dropped in, he wants an LED in the face of a cartoon figure on the front of the box to light up.

He seems to know nothing about electronics, but he has thought up some switches that close for a split second when money is dropped on to them.

Looking at his drawings, and using the capacitor-delay circuit, you are asked to design and make a money-box to show the toymaker what is possible.

Some questions to think about:

1 How far under the coin slot should the switch be?
2 Where will the circuit go?
3 How will you get access to the money?

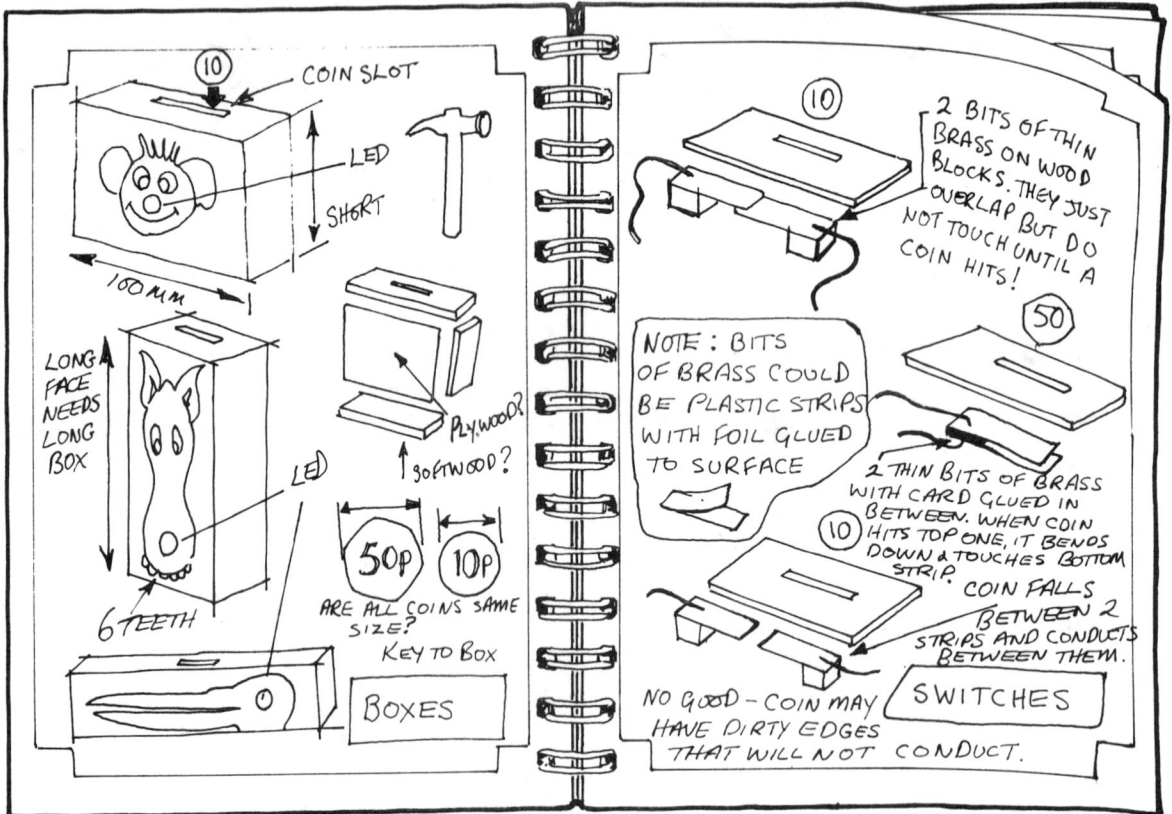

Questions

Test Yourself So Far

1 When capacitors are connected in parallel, their values are added to give the total. What is the total value of these capacitors connected in parallel?
How would they be drawn in the capacitor-delay circuit diagram?

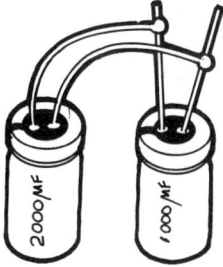

2 What happens if a second resistor is added into the delay circuit as shown?

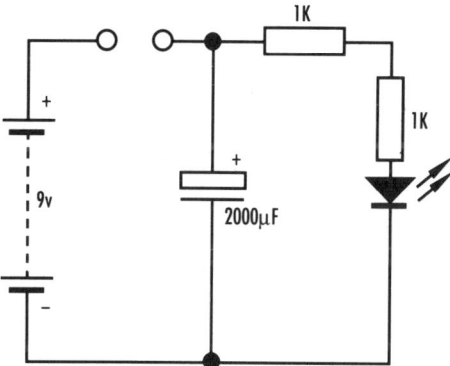

3 Can you spot the deliberate mistakes in the circuit diagram shown?

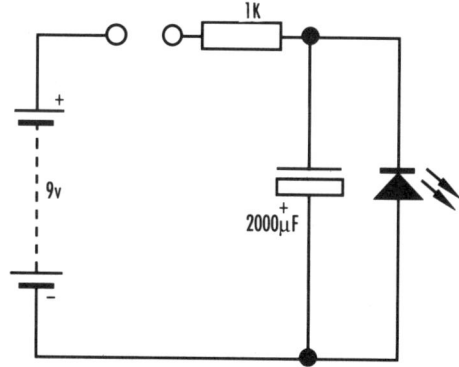

4 Can you work out what happens in this circuit?
(**Note:** The current does not flow *through* a capacitor; it fills up and then stops when fully charged.)

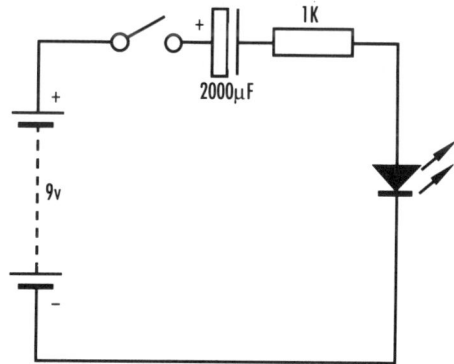

The Circuit Game

Rules of the Game

Besides being enjoyable, games can teach you a lot and help with revision. The circuit game aims to do all these things: you need luck – and some knowledge!

First of all, either photocopy or trace the game 'board' opposite. The idea of the game – for two, or even more players – is to draw lines (connections) between the contact points so that an LED would light up. The first person to draw a complete path from (+) to (−) connecting up an LED and resistor wins.

Rules

1 Each player uses a different-coloured pen.
2 Each player throws a dice and the number shown is the number of drawn links between points on the board the player can make.
3 The links must be up or across – never diagonal.
4 Players can link up to the same points but cannot share the same components; nor can they use the links another player has drawn.
5 No player can use 'spoiling' tactics by drawing in lines at random. Each player can only draw in lines as part of a *continuous* path.
6 The components must be linked up so that the circuit would work in practice – for example, the LED is the correct way around and a resistor is in series with it.

A sample game is shown below, won by the dotted-line player with a total of 14 drawn links.

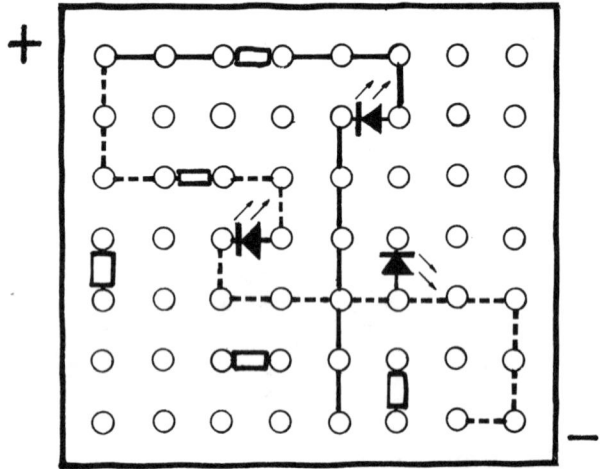

More Circuit Games

Perhaps you can now invent your own circuit games? Try drawing the game board but with the components removed. Put in your own components, and alter the rules as you think fit. For example, a small change that would make the game more difficult would be the use of lower-value resistors so that the path had to be through two rather than just one resistor.

Can you think of a way of generating 'random' numbers using your calculator instead of a dice?

Game Board

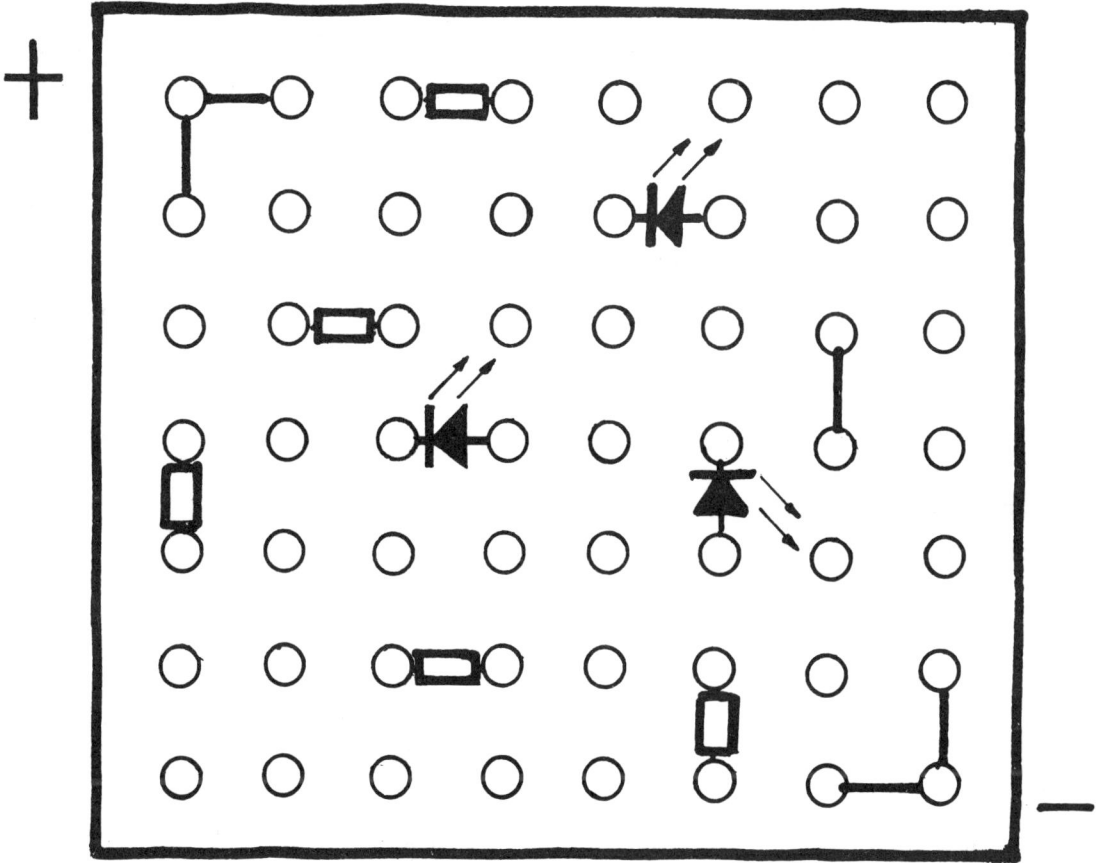

5 The Transistor

What Transistors Do

The **transistor** is really the miracle component of electronics. It has been around for only three decades, but has changed our world. (It was invented only just before Elvis Presley made his first record!)

Like models of cars, there are thousands of different transistors that do the same sort of job. We shall be working with only one called BC108. Like other transistors of its type, it has three legs – an *emitter* (next to the tag), *collector* and *base*.

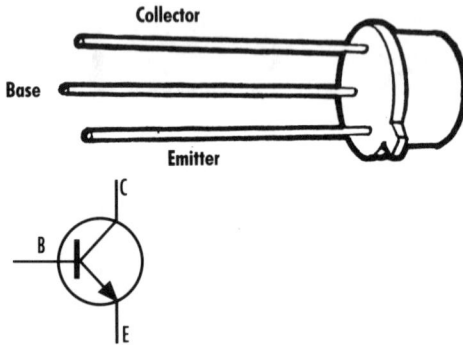

The transistor controls current in a very special way which is best explained in two steps. It will help you here to think of *conventional* current flow. This is the way the arrow-heads in the symbols point.

Step 1

If the collector and emitter legs of BC108 are connected as part of an LED circuit, nothing happens. The transistor is acting like a switch turned off.

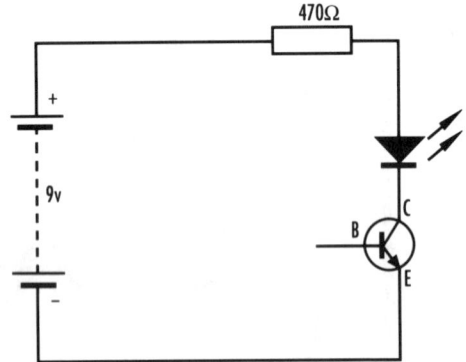

Step 2

To turn the transistor on, a small current has to flow between base and emitter. This can be supplied, for example, by a resistor. A very small base current flowing causes a much larger current to flow between collector and emitter, so that the LED lights up.

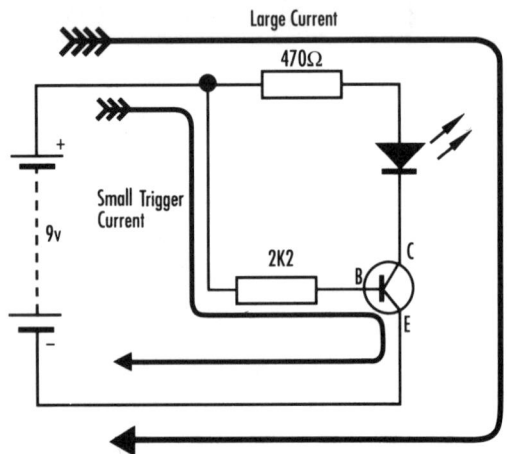

What Transistors Do

To be really sure about how the transistor works, try following the two current paths around on the diagram with the end of a pencil.

You might well ask at this point: why is a transistor needed to turn on an LED? The answer is that it gives us a very sensitive switch because so little base current is needed. So little, in fact, you can use your finger in place of the resistor – making the circuit a 'touch switch'.

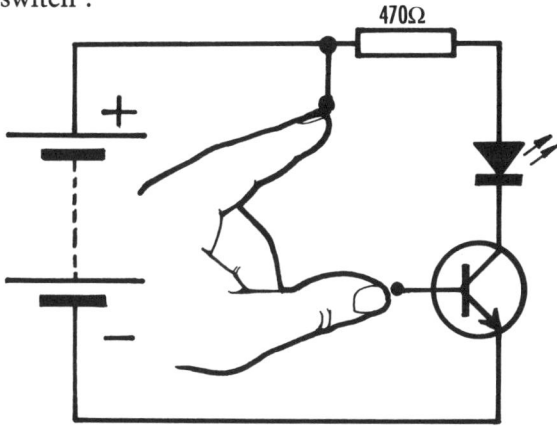

Make sure that the transistor is connected correctly! One easy way is to put it on its side with the tag pointing downwards. The base leg in the middle is left sticking out straight and the other two are bent outwards.

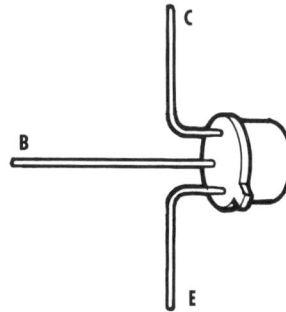

Experiment 3

Make up the transistor circuit on a wooden block (or by one of the other methods). Using the flying leads, you will be able to find out what sort of materials pass enough base current to turn the transistor on and light up the LED. The 2K2 resistor is needed to stop too much base current harming the transistor if you accidentally touch the leads together.

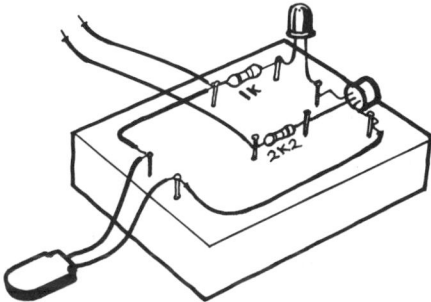

Transistor Projects

Project 12: Designing a Dampness Indicator

When thinking about buying a house, most people are unable to tell if the inside walls are damp.

The transistor circuit is a good indicator of dampness if the flying leads are connected to two small probes (about 20 mm apart) pressed into the wall. It will act only as a guide because walls contain different amounts of salts that will affect conduction. But at least it could alert the buyer to possible dampness problems.

You are asked to design and make a small dampness indicator for use by prospective house buyers. It must be small and portable and should not damage walls, apart from leaving two tiny indents from the probes.

Points to think about:

1 Should the probes be on leads or fixed to the device?
2 If the probes are sharp, how is the user protected when carrying the device?
3 Is this the sort of product that could be mass produced by injection moulding?
(See page 53 for ways of making models that look like real manufactured products.)

Transistor Projects

Project 13: Designing a Water-Level Alarm

As you may have found, water is a conductor for base current. If the two probes of the previous circuit are dipped into water, even at a distance apart, the LED will light up.

This means that it can be used as a warning device if an unseen tank, such as one in the roof, starts overflowing. The circuit is put where the LED can be seen, and a long pair of leads taken to probes in the tank.

A small buzzer could be used in place of the LED, but the probes would then have to be quite close together. This is because a buzzer needs more current than an LED and so there would have to be more base current to turn the transistor on more fully. (It is also a good idea to add a diode to this circuit to conduct away from BC108 the high voltage currents some buzzers produce.)

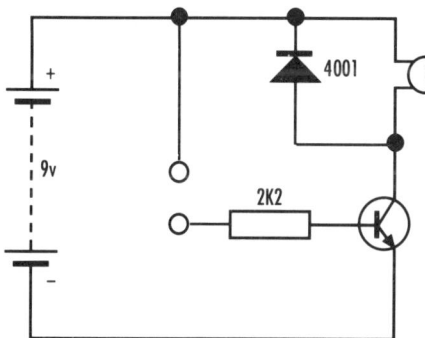

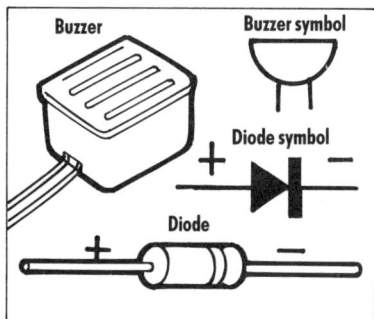

You are asked to design and make a water-level alarm to give an overflow warning for one of the following:
- Bath left to fill up
- Cellar which floods in heavy rain
- Child's paddling pool left to fill up
- Hot liquid poured into a cup by a blind or partially sighted person

Transistor Projects

Some points to think about:

1 Is an LED or buzzer to be used?
2 How far apart should the probes be? What should they be made from?
3 How will the probes/alarm be fixed? Will the probes just clip on?

(See Chapter 8 for notes on model making.)

Fact File

The resistance of our skin gets lower the more we perspire. This resistance is one of the things measured by the Polygraph, or lie detector, widely used in the USA. If you tell a lie, you tend to perspire a little more because of the stress – and this is picked up by the machine.

Graphite Lines and the Transistor

Experiment 4

You may already have thought of trying a pencil line to conduct base current to the transistor. A heavy graphite line, drawn by a soft pencil, will do the job, and that means you can actually *draw* part of a circuit instead of using wires or resistors!

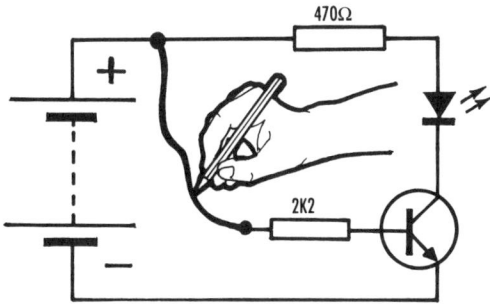

This gives you the chance to do some exciting work in graphics as well as electronics.

Before thinking about the next project, you must know how to join wires to graphite lines. Here are the tips to avoid failure:

1 Use only soft 3B or 4B pencils for the lines and go over them several times until very black.

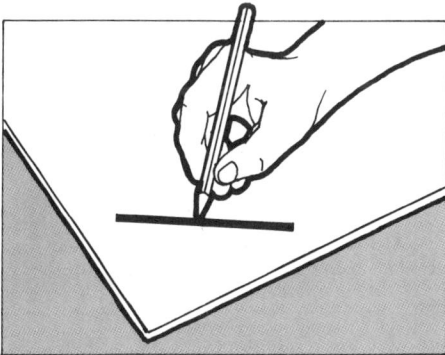

2 Wires joined to the graphite lines must be *stranded*.
3 Where the line joins the wire, it should be wider.

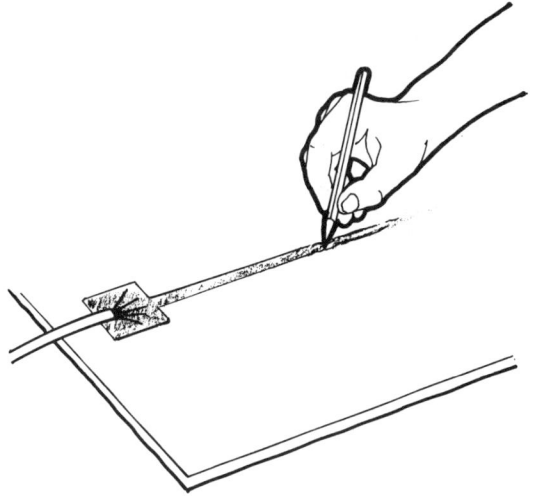

4 Stick down the stripped wire with Sellotape and tape extra wire down so that it will not easily pull off.

A Graphite Line Game

Project 14: A Graphite Line Game

Make up the transistor circuit on a wooden block or by one of the other methods and attach two flying leads. Connect one of these to the graphite line, as explained above, and then hold the end of the second lead in contact with the line. The LED should light up. If not, check the connection with the line and/or make the line darker.

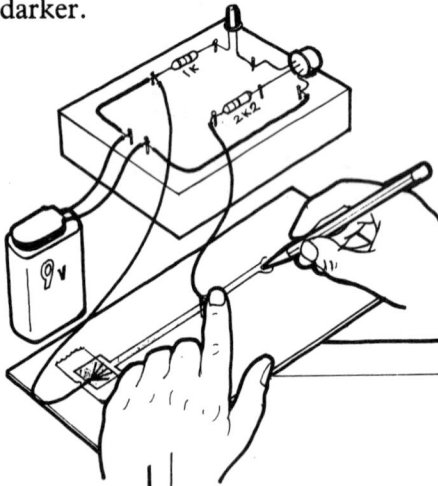

You should now be able to solve many interesting problems. Here is one:

A firm which makes games would like to sell a modern version of the old Pin-the-Tail-on-the-Donkey blindfolded party game. The firm can mass-produce the circuit in a small case and it can print on paper with a special graphite ink. The managing director's drawing shows what the firm has in mind, but he is not sure what it should look like or how it is played. Can you help by designing and making the paper part of the game? (Use the circuit made up for the experiment to prove that it works.)

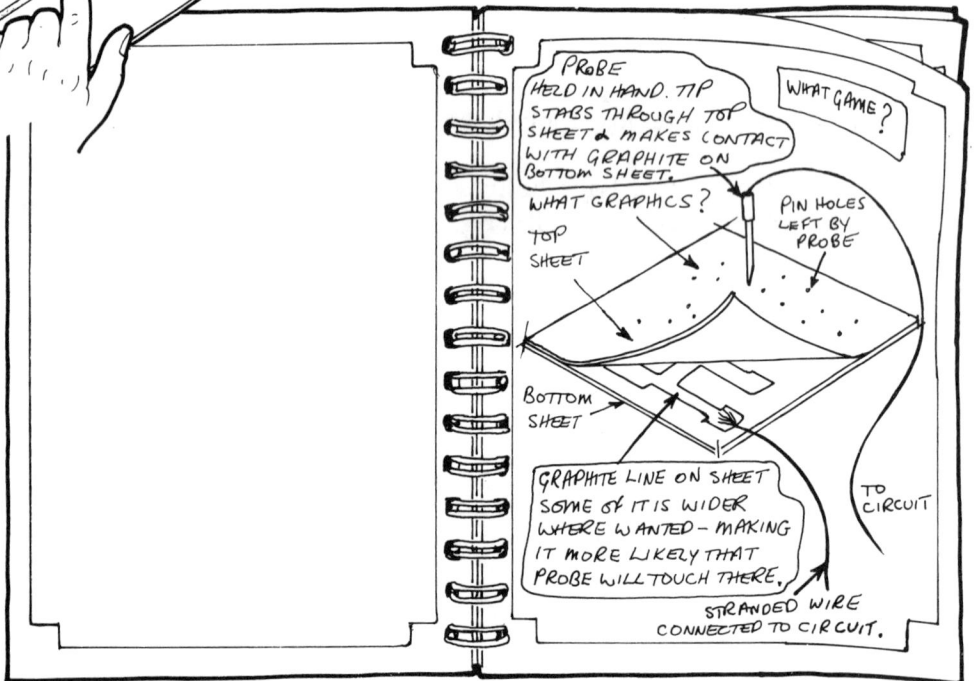

PROBE HELD IN HAND. TIP STABS THROUGH TOP SHEET & MAKES CONTACT WITH GRAPHITE ON BOTTOM SHEET.

WHAT GAME?

WHAT GRAPHICS?

TOP SHEET

PIN HOLES LEFT BY PROBE

BOTTOM SHEET

GRAPHITE LINE ON SHEET SOME OF IT IS WIDER WHERE WANTED – MAKING IT MORE LIKELY THAT PROBE WILL TOUCH THERE.

TO CIRCUIT

STRANDED WIRE CONNECTED TO CIRCUIT.

Transistor Timer Circuit

Experiment 5: A Transistor Timer

Adding a capacitor to the transistor circuit can
delay the LED (or buzzer) turning off for some
time.

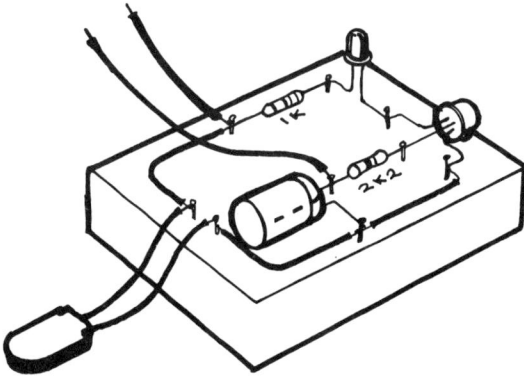

As before, when the flying leads are brought
together, BC108 turns on and the LED lights
up. But now, in a split second, the capacitor
charges up as well. When the leads are parted,
the capacitor acts as a small battery, supplying
the transistor with base current until it is
empty.

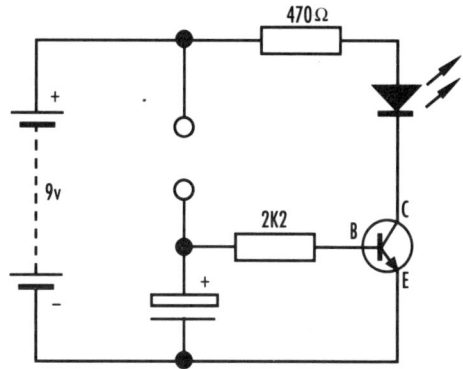

Using the circuit already made up or another
one, you can experiment with different-value
capacitors to find out how this affects the time
the LED or buzzer stays on.

Try the following values:
1 470μF
2 1,000μF
3 2,000μF

Does the LED/buzzer stay on for longer or for
less time with a bigger capacitor? Why is this?
You could also try adding extra resistors to it
and noting the effect this has.

With a 1,000μF capacitor, try the following
additional resistors:
1 2K2
2 4K7
3 10K

What is the problem with this circuit as a timer?
(*Clue*: What happens when the LED goes out?)

Transistor Alarm Circuits

Project 15: Building a Burglar Alarm

The transistor circuit with buzzer and capacitor added also makes a simple burglar alarm. The leads have only to be touched together quickly for BC108 to turn on for some time, and this is what we want from an alarm.

A burglar alarm gives a warning when one or more switches are closed – and it *stays* on even when the switch(es) is open again. Our circuit does just this, and it can be shown by connecting a mat switch (see Project 8 on p26) to the flying leads.

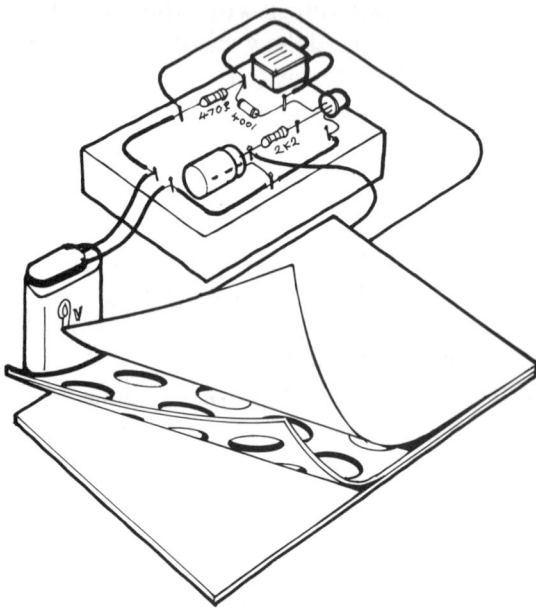

This circuit stops making a noise when the capacitor is empty or discharged, but this is what most alarms are designed to do. They frighten the thief away first and turn themselves off sometime later.

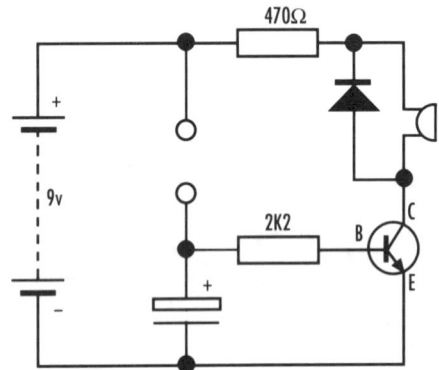

One of the most important parts of an alarm is the switch or switches that set it going.

There are two other types of switches that can be used in an alarm.

1 If the alarm is to be set going by shaking or vibration, a 'trembler' switch is needed. In the example shown, a small ball bearing or piece of metal is wedged into the top of a spring connected to one circuit lead. The other lead is taken to a copper tube around the spring, but insulated from it. When the switch is shaken, the spring will bend and its top contact on the inside of the tube.

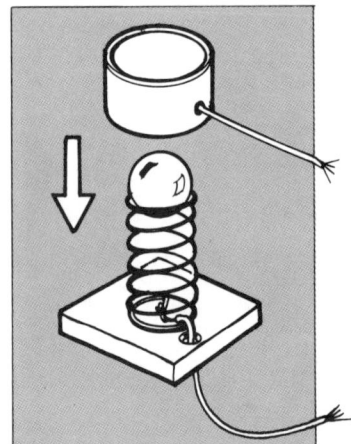

Transistor Alarm Circuits

2 If the alarm is to be set going by tilting at an angle, a 'pendulum' switch can be made. For example, a small metal weight hanging on the end of some stranded wire will touch on to another contact when tilted.

Using ideas like these, you should be able to design and make your own switches. The important thing is that they should be reliable and work every time.

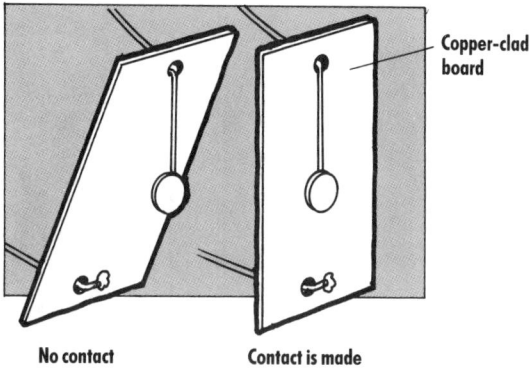

Copper-clad board

No contact   Contact is made

Using the transistor/capacitor circuit as your starting-point, design and make an alarm for one of the following:
1 Protection against theft of a brief-case or luggage case.
2 Protection to the entrance for one room in a house.
3 Warning that a ladder is tilting too far from upright.

Some points to think about:
1 Is the alarm to be portable or fixed in one place?
2 Is the switch inside the alarm itself or connected with leads?
3 How is the alarm switched off when not in use? Will an ordinary on/off switch need to be hidden?

The Transistor

Questions

Test Yourself So Far

1 Can you spot the deliberate mistakes in the diagram shown?

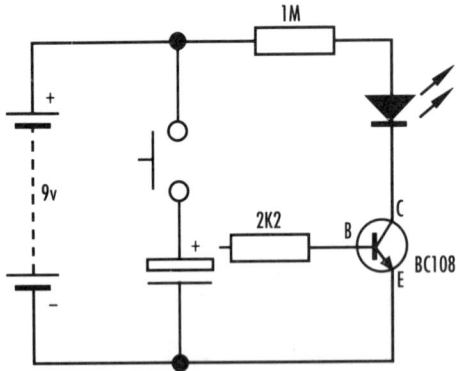

2 Which of the following are switches whose names have appeared so far: tremblo, rocker, slide, watch, mat, toggle, button, trembler, tilt, membrane, gill?

3 Which of the above switches could you use to set off an alarm in the following cases: (a) car being stolen (b) camera case being snatched (c) tractor in danger of tipping over?

4 Which of the two capacitors shown would keep the buzzer running for a longer time in the circuit on page 44?

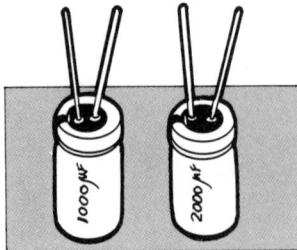

5 What is meant by 'surface mounting'?

6 What are the symbols for the buzzer and diode? (Try before looking!)

7 What would it take on the outside of a house to complete this rain alarm?

6 The SCR

What the SCR Does

The SCR (silicon controlled rectifier) behaves a bit like the transistor, but with one big difference: once turned on, it stays on.

The SCR has three legs, like the transistor, but they have different names – *gate* instead of base, *anode* instead of collector and *cathode* instead of emitter.

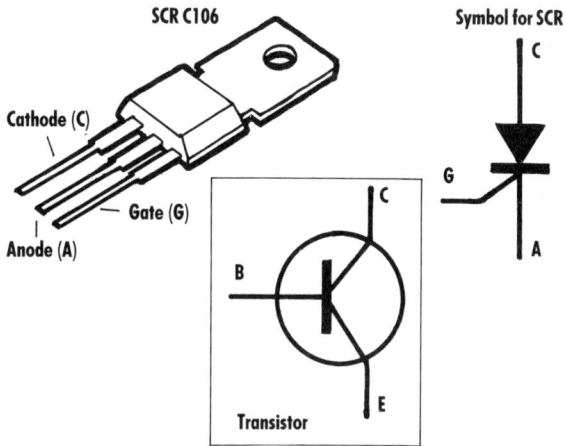

It is helpful to think about how the SCR works in two steps:

Step 1

When the anode and cathode of the SCR are connected into a simple LED circuit, current cannot flow. To begin with, the SCR is like a switch turned off.

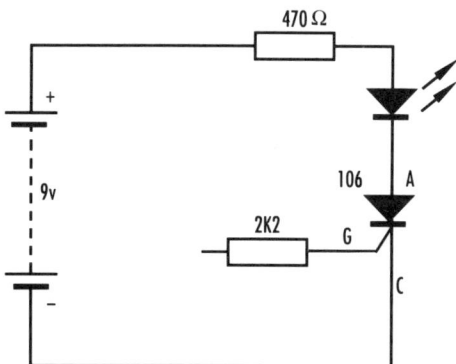

Step 2

A *small* current flowing to the gate through a resistor will cause the SCR to turn on and a larger current will flow from the anode to the cathode (conventional current flow). Unlike the transistor, this larger current will keep flowing even if the gate current is stopped.

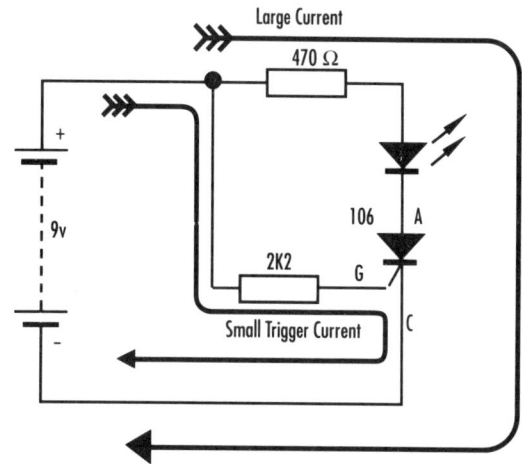

To make the SCR turn on, only the tiniest and shortest 'burst' of gate current is needed. The SCR is then said to be 'triggered'. This can even be done by quickly brushing a finger across it.

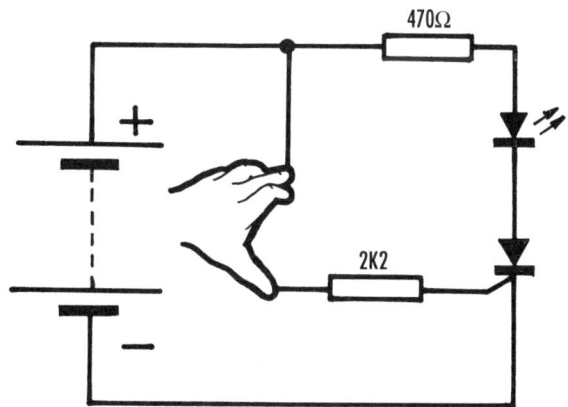

SCR Circuits

The problem is to turn the SCR off again! To do this, all current has to be stopped, if only for a split second. The battery could be disconnected, for example, or a switch in the circuit opened. When reconnected to the battery, the SCR can only be turned on again by another 'burst' of gate current.

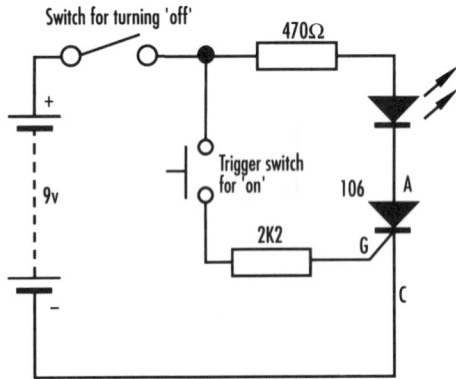

Another way of turning the SCR off is to *bypass* it very briefly. This means getting current to flow around it rather than through it. A wire connected between anode and cathode will do this – stealing current from the SCR and turning it off – even though the battery remains connected.

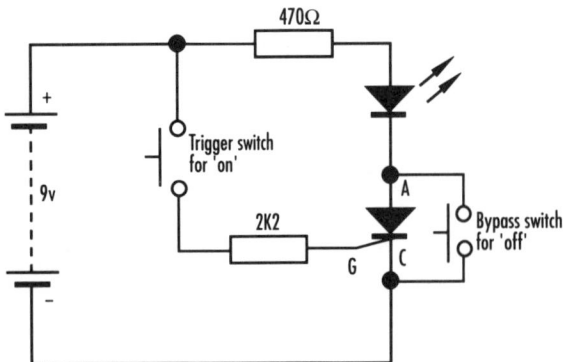

Like transistors, there are many different SCRs. SCR 106 is a very cheap one, and it can pass as much as 3 amps anode to cathode when triggered. (Compare this with BC108's $\frac{1}{10}$ amp collector to emitter!)

In a practical circuit, the gate must be protected with a resistor and if the SCR is passing a large current, it will get hot and needs fixing to a heat sink.

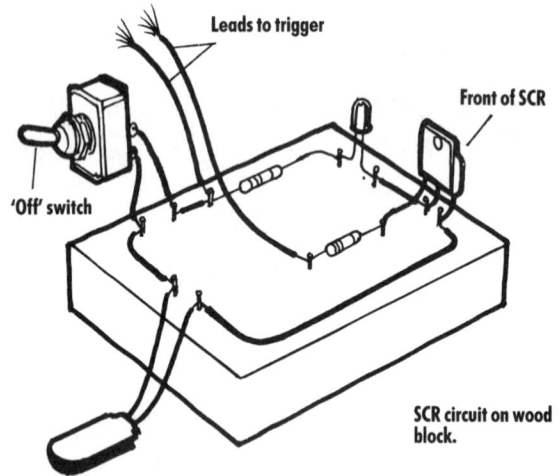

SCR circuit on wood block.

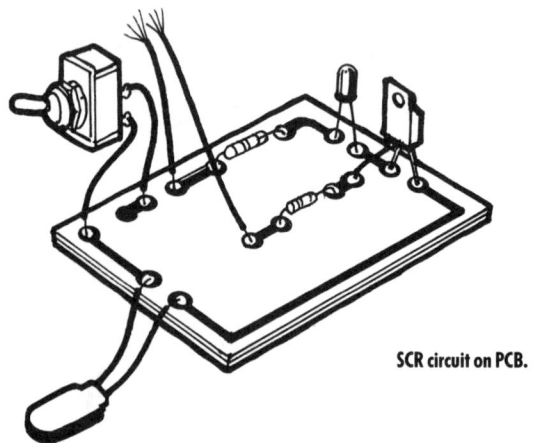

SCR circuit on PCB.

SCR Projects

Project 16: SCR Circuits

The SCR is ideal for alarm circuits because, once triggered, it will keep a buzzer (or bell) running. Unlike the transistor/capacitor circuit, it will do this until the battery goes flat or is disconnected.

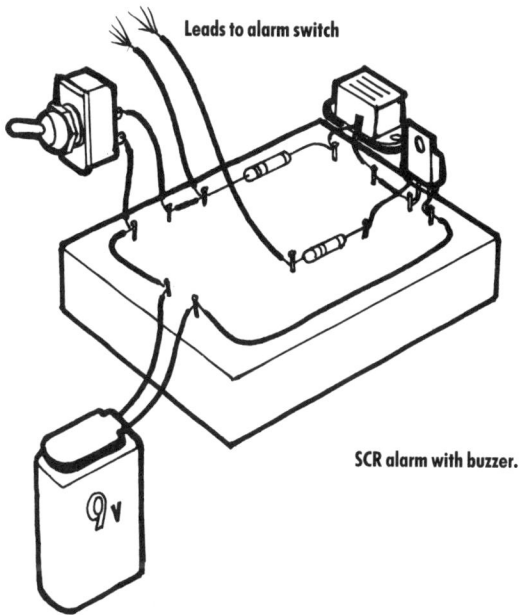

Leads to alarm switch

SCR alarm with buzzer.

All the switches looked at in this book will trigger an SCR alarm. There are other ways too, since the gate-triggering current will pass through water, damp materials, graphite, etc.

This means that the SCR could be used in some of the previous projects in place of other components. For example, there could be no arguments if it were used in the electronic wire game (see page 31) because the LED would stay on after any contact.

Using the SCR circuit as your starting-point, can you now design an alarm or game?

Note: With some types of buzzer, the SCR may seem to turn off without cause. If so, connect a capacitor in parallel. This keeps the SCR supplied with current if the buzzer itself interrupts it.

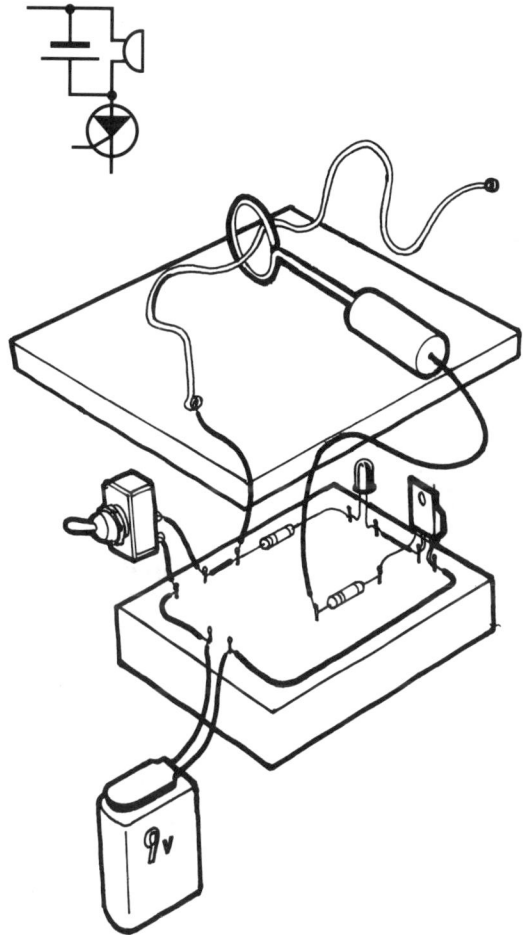

Action Chart

Start here

Follow this guide from the top. If any answer is NO, take action. If the circuit still fails to work, continue down the chart.

Is the circuit the same as the diagram?

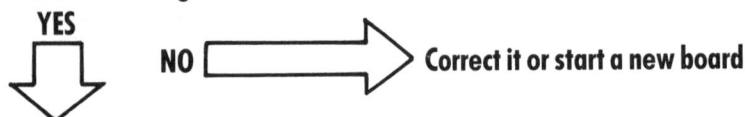

YES ↓   NO ⟹ Correct it or start a new board

Are the components the right way around?

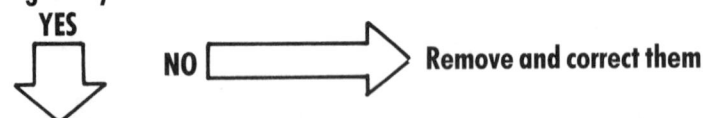

YES ↓   NO ⟹ Remove and correct them

Are all component values correct?

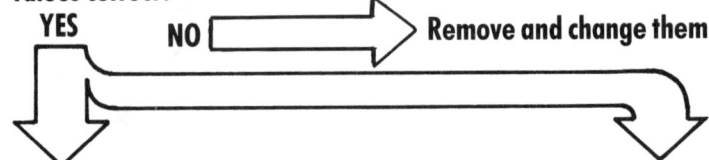

YES ↓   NO ⟹ Remove and change them

Wooden blocks

Are all the pins locked in?

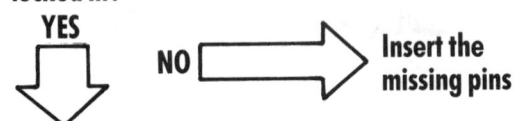

YES ↓   NO ⟹ Insert the missing pins

Is insulation on wires clear of the holes?

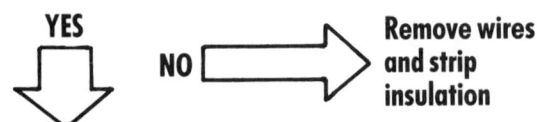

YES ↓   NO ⟹ Remove wires and strip insulation

Are pins tight in the holes?

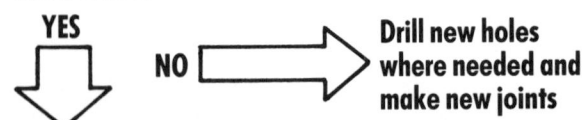

YES ↓   NO ⟹ Drill new holes where needed and make new joints

Soldered boards

Are all joints soldered?

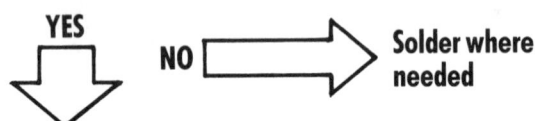

YES ↓   NO ⟹ Solder where needed

Are joints firm? (No wires or legs moving in join)

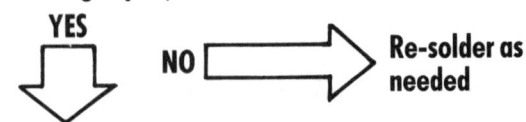

YES ↓   NO ⟹ Re-solder as needed

Have you made sure no solder runs across where it should not?

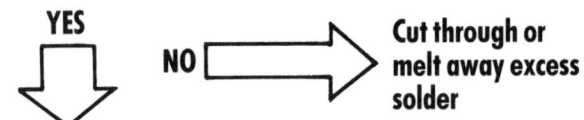

YES ↓   NO ⟹ Cut through or melt away excess solder

If circuit still fails to work, continue on to the next page of tests.

Testing for Continuity

Continuity Testing

Even if the circuit joints *look* good, they might not be making contact. To find out if the current path is continuous between any two points, we can use the first LED circuit (see page 15).

If there is a problem with this or it is not available, one can be quickly made up by soldering or using a terminal block to connect the parts.

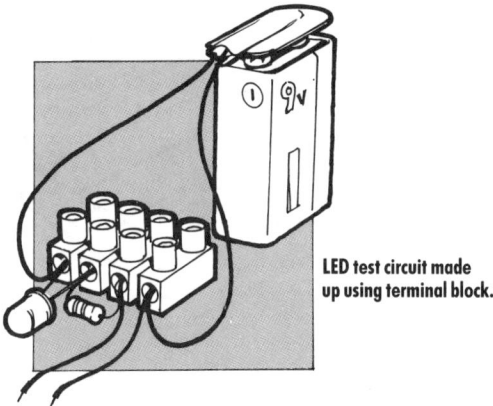

LED test circuit made up using terminal block.

Tester circuit

Points to test between

When testing a circuit, take nothing for granted – including the battery snap. This example shows you how to test the capacitor-delay circuit (see page 30), but the same rules apply to the others.

First, offer one probe to the snap (+) and the second to each joint in turn up to the leg of the first component. The circuit path is continuous as long as the LED keeps lighting up.

Do this also along the path from the snap (−). Finally, test between other joints in the circuit, making sure that you touch the probes on to the component legs.

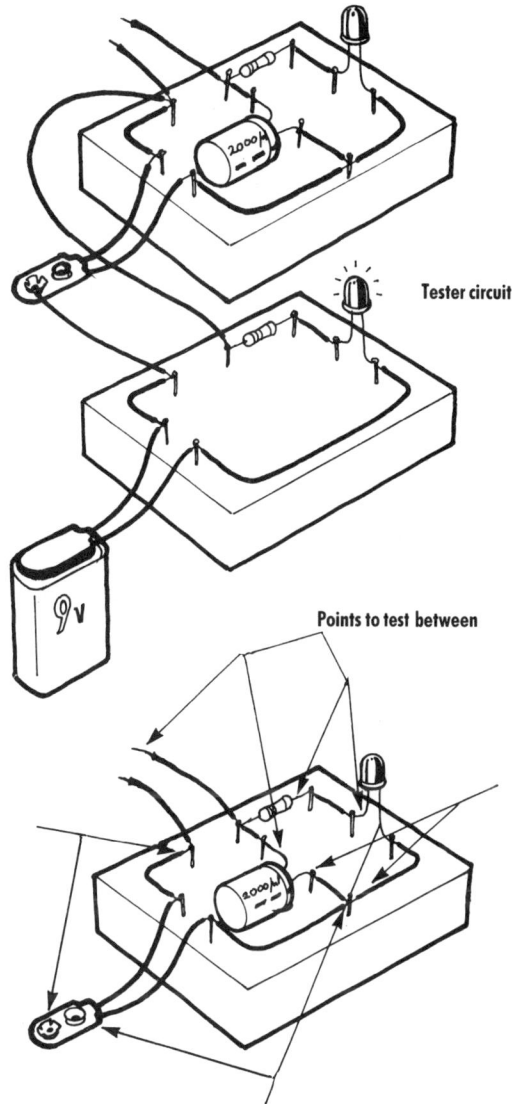

If no fault is found and the circuit still fails to work, ask your teacher to check the components with a meter.
Remember: Components are usually the last things to be faulty.

8 Making Product Models

Use of a Cassette Box

When products are designed for mass production, it is common for full-size models to be made so that ideas can be developed and discussed. These are sometimes very precise working models that are impossible to tell from the real thing.

If you keep to quite simple shapes, you can make professional looking models to contain the circuits in this book. All you have to know are a few simple tricks of the trade.

Use of Found Cases

To turn a circuit into a product, you have to package it in a case or shell. Sometimes, when you start modelling, ready-made plastic boxes can be used. They do not give much choice of shape, but they allow you to practise some of the modelling techniques that professionals use.

An empty cassette box is an ideal starting-point. They hinge open, and will house at least two AA-size batteries and other components, as well as giving two flat sides to work on.

Let us assume that the bulb/fuse tester is being packaged. First of all, the batteries have to be located and wires connected. As luck has it, two batteries will just slip into the lid where they can be wedged with folded brass strips at either end. The wires are soldered to these.

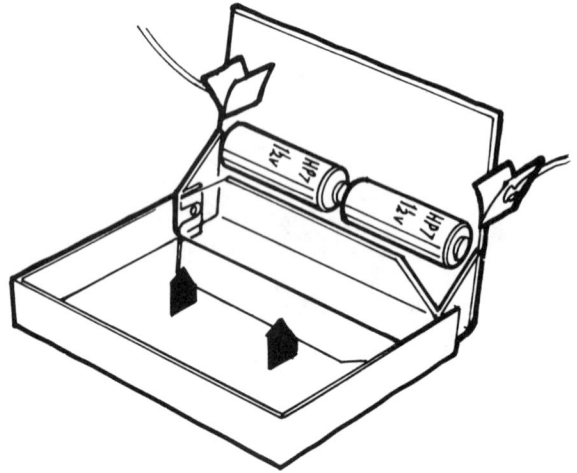

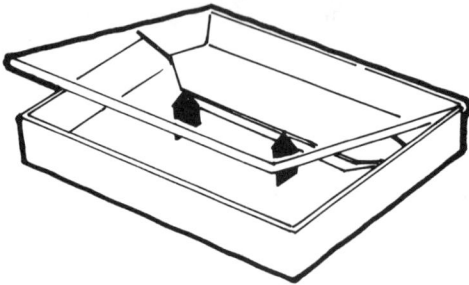

Use of a Cassette Box

If the components are not already soldered to a small PCB, they must be separately positioned in the box and connected when in place. For example, the LED could be bonded into a hole in one end of the box and a pair of studs (copper rivets, for example) in the lid. Connections are made by soldering in the resistor and *stranded* wires. These have to flex when the lid is opened.

Now the fun starts! Most products have relief details moulded in: for example, 3D logos and lettering and textures giving a look and 'feel' to the surface. You can produce these effects by applying self-adhesive stickers, cut-up address labels, Eddings' stick-on vinyl lettering – and many other things (all available from a stationer's). When sprayed with cellulose paint, they really look as if they are a moulded part of a coloured plastic surface.

Make sure that the labels are rubbed down hard with the back of a teaspoon – even if they look secure.

Finally, make sure that the paint is applied in several *very thin* coats.
Warning: Spray paint only in a well-ventilated place or in the open air.

When the paint is dry, rub-down lettering can give a really professional finish. Plan it well, use sparingly, and get it straight!

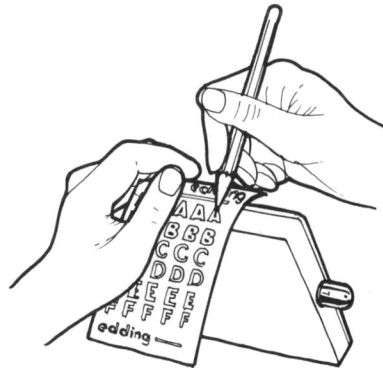

Making Your Own Case

Although the use of found cases gives practice at some modelling techniques, you do not have much freedom to design with them.

The next step is to make your own cases, using a few pieces of sheet polystyrene and its adhesive – both of which are stocked by good model shops.

Polystyrene sheet

For a simple rectangular case, the first job is to decide on the sizes of all pieces before cutting them up. Thick sheet, 3 mm for the sides and 2 mm for front and back, allows you to make a wide glue joint on the edges. (Make sure you allow overlap all around.)

'Cut' the sheet by scoring along it against a steel ruler with a scriber (or hook-shaped tool) and then breaking along this line over the edge of a table or in a vice.

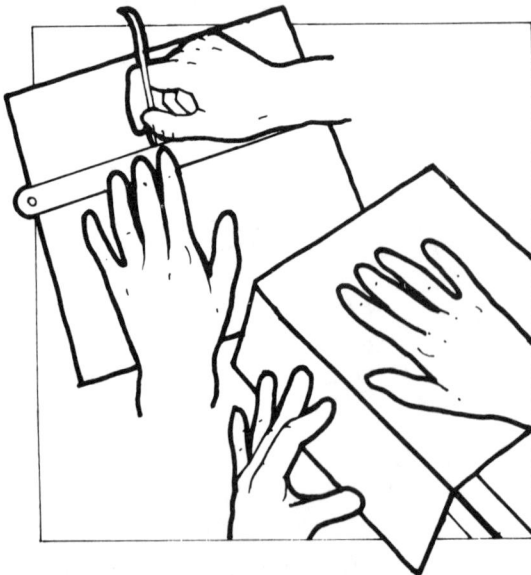

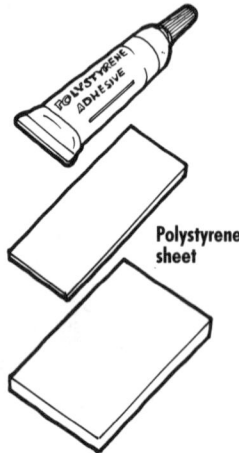

The edges are then smoothed on wet-and-dry abrasive paper with the polystyrene kept upright against wooden blocks to make sure the edges are at 90° to the faces.

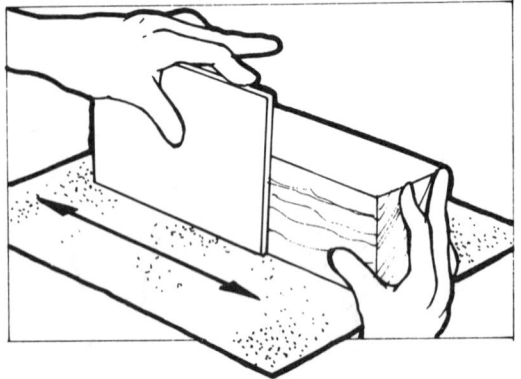

Using a *small* amount of glue, put together the main case and glue in end-pieces for extra length. These are also used for fastening the back on – either with small pads of double-sided tape or self-tapping screws.
(**Note:** A small chamfer around the edge of the back will look like the breakline found on mass-produced products.)

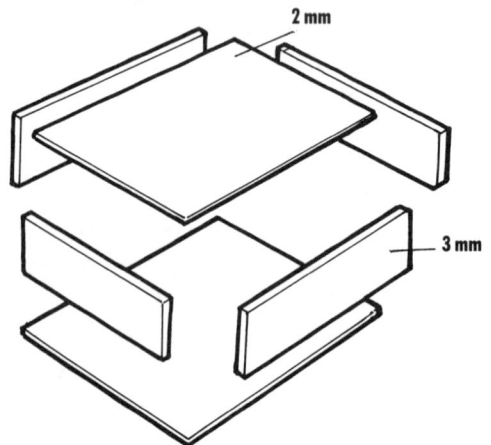

2 mm

3 mm

Making Your Own Case

The completed case is rubbed down on very
fine wet-and-dry paper. Any gaps are filled
with cellulose putty filler for car bodies before a
final rubbing-down.

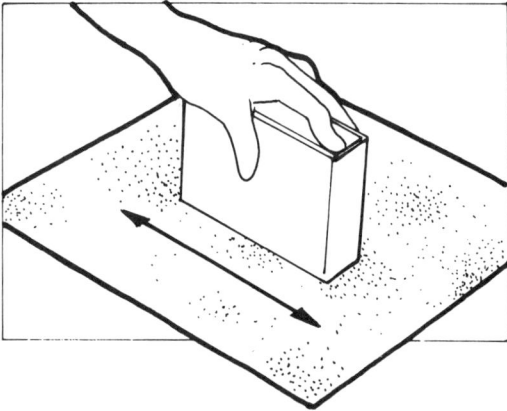

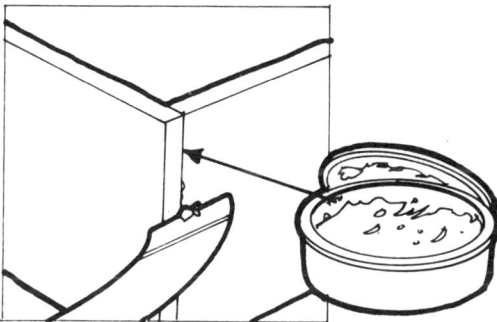

If the case needs holes to let the sound out from
a buzzer, these can be drilled through matrix
board, a form of circuit board, which is used
here as a drill jig. It is taped to the model's
surface and the holes are then drilled through.

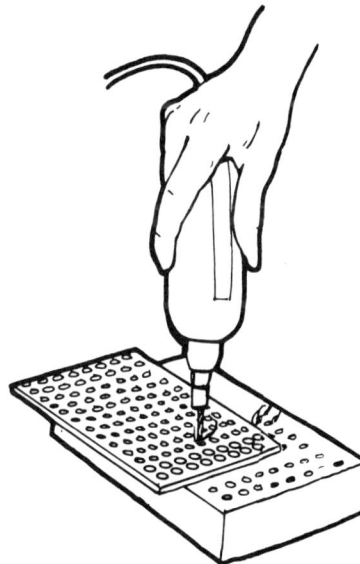

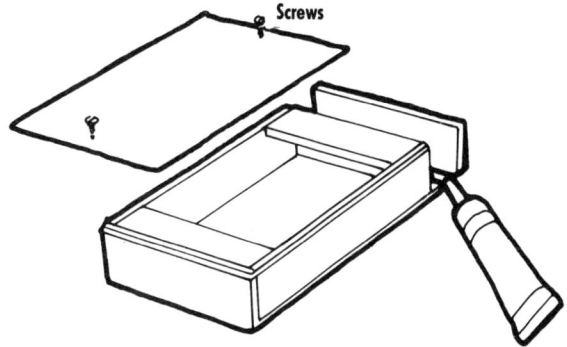

Making Your Own Case

As before, relief details should be put on before spraying. Cellulose paint does not stick very well to polystyrene, and so you must try to ensure that the surface is good before painting. If you do have to rub it down again with fine wet-and-dry paper, make sure that the paint has been left at least 48 hours.

9 Ohm's Law

Many people think that electronics is full of mathematics. In fact, much of what goes on is just simple arithmetic, using something called **Ohm's Law**.

Ohm's Law tells us how current, voltage and resistance in a circuit are related to one another. If we can put a figure to two of these things, we can work out the third without having to measure it.

When we use Ohm's Law, voltage is written as V, resistance as R and current as I.

Ohm's Law states that:
Voltage = current × resistance   V = I × R
Current = voltage ÷ resistance   I = V/R
Resistance = voltage ÷ current   R = V/I
An easy way of remembering these is to think of
$$\frac{V}{I\,R}$$
Take away the one you want to know, and the position of the other two tells you whether to multiply or divide.

Let us look at some examples of Ohm's Law. It can be used to work out how much current flows in the LED circuit shown on page 15. This is I = V/R.
I = 9/470 = 0.019 or 19 mA (19/1000 of an amp).
This is about the maximum current the LED can safely handle.

In the circuit below, a tiny loudspeaker is being used for continuity testing. Instead of an LED lighting up when the circuit is completed, a click is heard. If the current flowing must not exceed 40 mA to avoid damaging the loudspeaker, what value resistor should be used in the circuit? (Clue: R = V/I.)

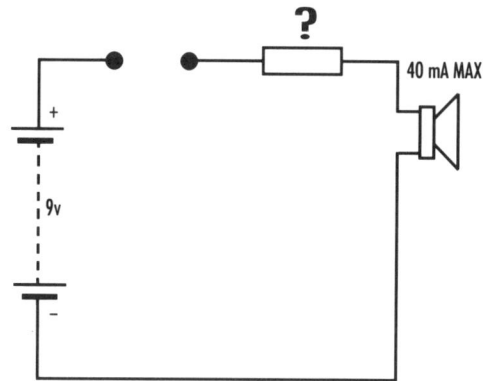

Amp Short for Ampère. The unit of electrical current named after a French mathematician and physicist.

Amplify To make larger.

Battery A number of cells (*see* Dry Cell) added together to produce a higher voltage.

Capacitor A component which can be used as a small store or reservoir for current.

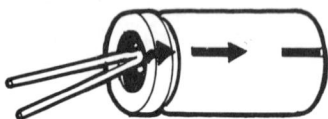

Carbon A very common material used in making resistors. It is mixed with other materials to let more or less current pass through it.

Ceramics Materials, like most china cups and saucers, which are excellent insulators, especially for high voltages.

Circuit A combination of conductors and components that conduct and control current.

Components The parts making up a circuit.

Conductor A material that passes current with very little resistance.

Conventional Current Flow The opposite to electron flow in a circuit. It was originally believed that a 'fluid' flowed from $(+)$ to $(-)$. This idea was found to be incorrect when the electron was discovered. But it was too late to change the way we spoke about and described current flow. When talking about current flow, you must make it clear that you mean either electron flow $(-)$ to $(+)$ or conventional current flow: the assumption that something is flowing the other way.

Diode A component that allows current to pass through it only in one direction.

Dry Cell A chemical device for producing current. The chemicals are not really dry but in paste form. Where several are put together in series we have a battery.

Electron Materials are made up of atoms and these in turn contain one or more electrons. When moving through conductors as electric current, you might think of electrons as dodgem cars bumping each other along.

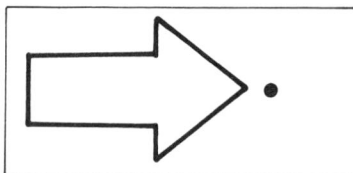

There are billions of electrons in the ink of this full stop.

Electronics The subject concerned with the control of electrons in circuits.

Farad The unit of capacitance. One farad is too large a unit to use in electronics, so we use microfarads (1 millionth of a farad), picofarads (1 thousand millionths of a farad), and nanofarads (1 million millionths of a farad). Abbreviations: µF, pF, nF.

Flux *See* Solder.

Graphite A form of carbon which conducts current and behaves just like a resistor.

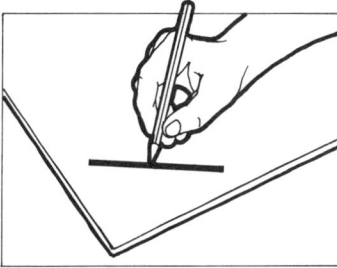

Heat Sink Something for taking away unwanted heat. Pliers, for example, can be used as a heat sink during a soldering operation.

Insulator A material that does not normally pass current. Glass and ceramic materials are excellent insulators and were used as such before plastics were developed.

LED Short for Light Emitting Diode, a device that emits light when current flows through it in the right direction.

Matrix Board A plastic board with regularly spaced holes to hold pins on which components are soldered. A matrix board can also be used as a drill jig for model making.

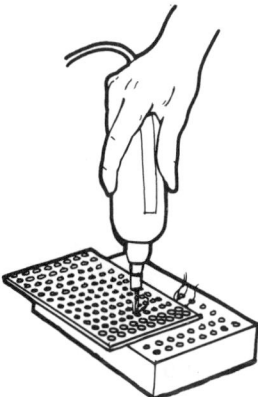

Membrane Panel A type of switch made up of a sandwich of thin plastic layers, at least two of which are printed with conductors. When these very thin switches are pressed in the right place, conductors in different layers meet.

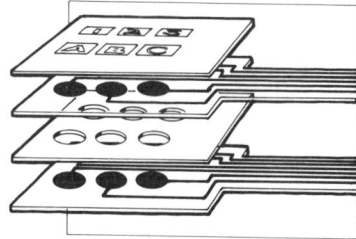

Ohm The unit of resistance, named after the German, George Ohm.

Ohm's Law The law of physics that states the relationship between current, voltage and resistance. If two of these are known, the third can be worked out using Ohm's Law.

Parallel A method of connecting components together. When connected in parallel, two or more components are connected identically between the same points of a circuit. Two resistors connected in parallel, for example, can be placed side by side and their legs joined together at either end. These give two routes for current to take and the total resistance they offer is less than either one alone.

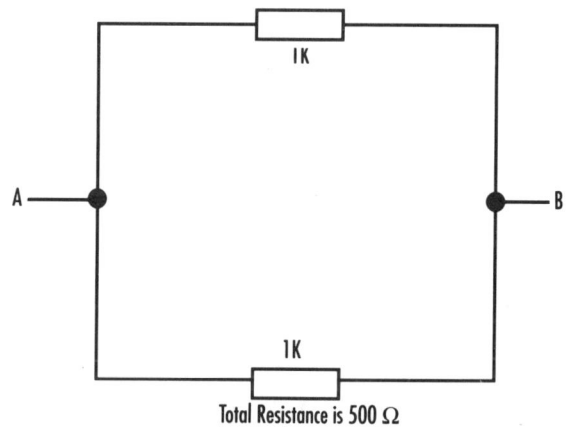

Total Resistance is 500 Ω

Mini-Dictionary

PCB Short for Printed Circuit Board, a board having thin copper tracks for connecting components.

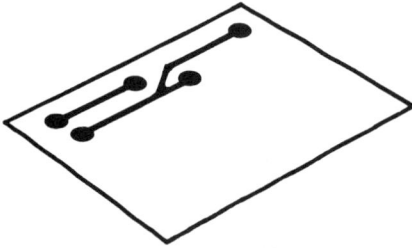

Polystyrene A plastic material often used in sheet form for vacuum forming.

Resistor A device which acts against current flowing freely. The wire element of an electric fire resists flow of current and gets hot – as does the filament of a light bulb.

SCR Short for Silicon Controlled Rectifier, a member of the thyristor family of components, generally used for controlling large currents. When triggered with a small current, the SCR turns on and continues to conduct until its current supply is interrupted.

Series A method of connecting components together. They are connected in a line, like the carriages of a train. Resistors are often connected in series to reduce current flow. Two light bulbs connected in series to a battery will glow dimmer than just one, since two present more resistance to current flow than one.

$$1K \qquad 1K$$
A ———[   ]———[   ]——— B
Total Resistance is 1K + 1K = 2K

Snap The clip that attaches to the top of some batteries.

Solder The solder used in electronics work is normally an alloy, or mixture, of tin and lead which has a low melting-point. As well as melting at a low temperature, it is made to go solid again quickly after melting. It normally has a resin flux as fine threads in its centre (multi-core solder) which flows out over the hot joint to assist the solder fusing.

Surface Mounting (SM) A method of mounting components on PCBs. Both the copper connecting tracks and the components are placed on the same side of the board.

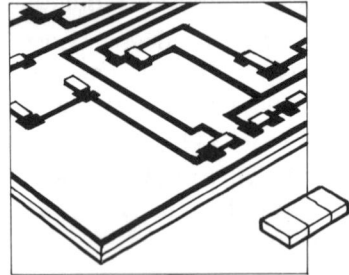

Switch A component used in circuits for controlling current flow by allowing it to pass or preventing it, or altering the path it takes.

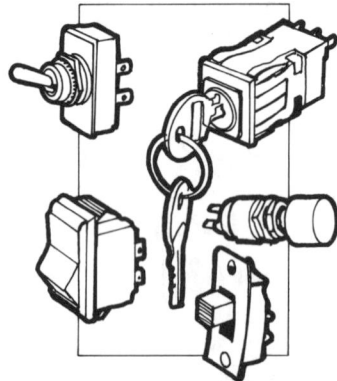

Symbol In electronics a symbol is a 'picture' on paper that stands for a component.

Tinning The application of a thin film of solder to metal surfaces to be joined by soldering.

Tinning ensures all surfaces are coated and makes joining easier.

Transistor A component, invented only in 1948, that can be used as an amplifier of current or as a switch. A small current to its base causes a larger current to flow between collector and emitter.

Volt The unit of voltage named after the Italian Volta. Until quite recently, voltage was often referred to as pressure.

Wire A conductor, usually made of copper and wrapped with a PVC insulating sleeve. Two types are common in electronics. Stranded wire contains a number of fine copper wires which makes it flexible, and this is used for flying leads, battery connections, leads on appliances, etc. Single-core wire has only one conductor. It is normally used for connections where the wire will not be moved.

Index